Between Two Eter

Between Two Eternities

A HELEN WADDELL
ANTHOLOGY

EDITED BY

FELICITAS CORRIGAN osb

First published in Great Britain 1993
Society for Promoting Christian Knowledge
Holy Trinity Church
Marylebone Road
London NW1 4DU

British Library Cataloguing-in-Publication Data
A catalogue record for this book is available from the British Library

ISBN 0-281-04653-0

Typeset by Action Typesetting Limited, Gloucester
Printed in Great Britain by
Mackays of Chatham plc, Chatham, Kent

Contents

Part Four: PREACH THE GOSPEL TO EVERY CREATURE

Part Five: I WILL ALLURE AND BRING INTO THE WILDERNESS

Part Six: ONE GENERATION PASSETH AWAY

CONTENTS

Acknowledgements

Following a now familiar pattern, I acknowledge my debt above all and before all to Miss Mollie Martin, whose unbounded generosity has made possible the study of her aunt, Helen Waddell, that has taken various forms to convey 'the roll, the rise, the carol, the creation'. In addition I must thank two members of my own community: Dame Josephine Holden, whose quiet efficiency reduced chaos to order by arranging masses of undated letters in chronological sequence; and Dame Philippa Edwards, keen of intellect, valiant of heart, steadily mastering Helen's daunting assortment of stories, plays, poems, newspaper columns, academic monographs, medieval studies and personal letters. My trusty and trusted helper, Mrs Anna Rains, has been ever at hand in time of need; Mrs Mary Henderson readily interpreted our friendship, 'that most sacred thing' as Boethius calls it, in practical terms of proof-reading that prevented at least one serious blunder; Mrs Honor Sharman generously allowed me to include Helen's tribute to her uncle, Sir Basil Blackett KCB; and my publishing editor, Philip Law and his colleagues added finishing touches to the work. To all my debtors, I can only offer 'evermore thanks, the exchequer of the poor'.

F.C.

Note

The shape of this anthology has been determined by the contours of Helen Waddell's own mind. From childhood to old age, she was the embodiment of the psalmist's *annos aeternos in mente habui* – I have kept the eternal years in mind (Vulg. Ps.76.6). Steeped in the Bible by heredity and upbringing, cut off for ten years of her youth from human friendship and the arts, Helen underwent at the hands of her stepmother a spiritual *ascesis* as searing and formative as that of any Desert Father. It seems hardly surprising therefore that the bulk of her work should fall naturally into the Christological form that had shaped her own life. Each extract is summarized in a caption drawn from holy Scripture, viewed against an unchanging backcloth of Our Lord Jesus Christ, loving Redeemer of all the children of God.

F.C.

Introduction

Thee, God, I come from, to thee go,
All day long, I like fountain flow.

Gerard Manley Hopkins, trained in the school of Ignatius Loyola, has put into a nutshell the aim of all spiritual exercises: to live in the flux of time with eyes fixed on the eternal. The boundless, endless and sublime image of eternity has always haunted the mind of man. Henry Vaughan saw it as a great ring of calm light surmounting the vast shadow of time with its cycle of hours, days, years; Blake saw eternity in an hour; Shelley's vision looked into the space opening out within the freedom of God, and saw it as Life, the time for action that we call human history:

> Life, like a dome of many-coloured glass,
> Stains the white radiance of eternity
> Until death shatters it to fragments.

The Bible views time under different modes of temporality: the opening pages of Genesis reveal the time of paradise, when God conversed with man in the cool breath (the *pneuma*, the Holy Spirit) of the evening (Gen. 3.8). All too swiftly, the narrative then passes to the time of sin, to creation heading for disaster, when the Creator rejects his handiwork, 'whereby the world that then was, being overflowed with waters, perished' (2 Pet. 3.6). Hope returns with the time of the Old and New Covenants, converging upon and then fulfilled in Jesus Christ, Lord and Redeemer. Finally it reaches the time of all who, in and through Christ, renounce unreality, time lost and corrupted, space full of nothing, duration leading nowhere, empty annihilating time, 'having no hope and without God in the world' (Eph. 2.12). In other words, those who outsoar the shadow and enter into real time, wherein they once more encounter God, walk with him, and accept his will, his wisdom and his love.

During his life on earth, Christ constantly referred to his 'hour': 'Mine hour is not yet come'. That 'hour' does not belong to paradisal,

1

sinful, or to redeemed time – it stretches far beyond the narrow limits of salvation history to its very source in the Godhead, out of the history of the chosen people of Israel into that of the whole human race. Jesus Christ, incarnate son of God, stands for ever surrounded by his disciples and friends, men and women alike, Jews and Gentiles – not only with Israel, Assyria and Egypt, but also with Sodom and her daughters (Ezek. 16.55). By the power of the cross, he has levelled to the dust the wall of partition, and offered to all the freedom of heaven where, to add Milton's *Damon* to Shelley's *Adonais*,

> . . . the sound of the lyre and the voice of singing
> Kindle and quicken the dancing feet,
> Where the Bridegroom's feast is toward,
> And the mystic wine is poured,
> The madness and the ecstasy of Heaven.

This map of eternity and time has provided the ground plan for the following selection from the writings of Helen Waddell, many either unpublished or little known, some decipherable only by an expert palaeographer. The mystery of eternity was never far from her thoughts. At eight years of age, possessed of a little mind stocked with the entire Letter to Hebrews, she had climbed with bare toes up the knobbly bark of the maple tree in the garden of her Tokyo home, to shelter in the leafy gazebo of its branches and cudgel her brains over the anguish of the struggle in time. 'One remembers one's childish pondering over the strange refusal of the intimate sure sweetness of return to this world of sunlight and trees in the text: "Women received their dead raised to life again,"' she told Dr George Taylor many years later, ' "and others were tortured, not accepting deliverance, that they might obtain a better resurrection."' The concluding prayer on the first page of this anthology is a pure distillation of Helen Waddell's approach to God: she frequently quotes the opening phrase as if it had become the leitmotif of all her actions: . . . Lord, thy eternity dost ever besiege our life . . . All our life Thou hast sought us: seek us still. . . .

The prayer had been written in response to a request for a contribution to a book of prayers for use by the Girls' Auxiliary of Belfast – in the event, it was unceremoniously declined by the pious judges as being too difficult. The rejection was reported to her spiritual father in India with mingled anger and amused irony:

I did not change the prayer beginning 'Thy eternity dost ever besiege our life'. That was the only difficult sentence in it; and even that I left because by all means possible I wanted to hammer into the brain of your working-class girl some idea of eternity, if it were only the beauty of the word. For to get any conception of infinity is like taking the stone off the mouth of a well.

Therein perhaps lies the difficulty. Precisely how do human creatures come into live contact with the eternal God? Helen Waddell would reply unhesitatingly, 'By prayer!' She defined prayer as 'the electricity of the science of religion'. In 1908, when she went up to Queen's University filled with the spiritual ideals inherited from her long line of Presbyterian forebears, she had found a moribund Christian Union. Within a year, she and her friend Meta Fleming (who was to meet an early death as a missionary in India) had transformed it into the most flourishing student body in the college. It goes without saying that Helen was speedily voted president. Her first address entitled 'The Prayer Life of the Christian Union' opened with the uncompromising statement: 'The title of this paper is not the subject of it; and the paper of which it was the subject is in the fire.' Wrestling with the topic for three days had convinced her that Christ our Lord was not concerned with organizations: he was greatly concerned with individual souls: 'He calleth his sheep by name'. It is all too easy and perilous to shelter behind a plural pronoun. Religion is inseparable from the life of the unique person that every one is.

For three days our Lord preached in great patience to five thousand who had followed him into the wilderness; but think you that he felt anything of the uplift of heart with which he went through the streets of Jerusalem watching for the face of the man who had been cast out because he would not say that his healer was a sinner? And when he had found him he said unto him, 'Dost thou believe on the Son of God?' He answered and said, 'And who is he, Lord, that I might believe on him?' And Jesus answered him, 'Thou hast both seen him, and he it is who speaketh with thee.' Still do the multitudes throng and press him, and still he says, 'Who touched me?'

Helen herself was by no means unfamiliar with those searing 'touches of God' spoken of by the mystics.

'What if it were really true,' she wrote to her sister Meg, 'that the power at the back of this cruel universe were love as we know it? It's no wonder Dante said when he had that vision of "love that moves the sun and stars" that it was *tanto ottraggio,* a kind of outrage of his being.

3

For to come within the least whisper of it is to leave one gasping . . .
it is so terrible that one almost looks about for familiar little shelters
of noise and buses to shut out the stars.'

In youth she had warned the Christian Union at Queen's that prayer
did not consist in words, in reading about prayer, or in talking about it.
Prayer and daily life are woven into Christ's commandment: 'Love one
another as I have loved you.' Helen Waddell's writings are marvels of
theology lived, theology that would delight a saint and not repel a sinner.
When success crowned her work, it did not turn her head. In a letter to
her sister she quoted Oliver Goldsmith: 'Still to my brother turns with
ceaseless pain/And drags at each remove a lengthening chain.' She
added: 'You go up a hill when you're young, and think you will go on
walking into the westering sun. And then you find a precipice and a
valley of dry bones – and if one looks for him, I suppose, God.'

Inside the back cover of the American edition of *Beasts and Saints*
Helen's niece recently discovered an almost indecipherable pencilled
script obviously dashed off by the author. It reads:

> *In excessu mentis* – the contemplative ecstasy which to some comes
> only in prayer, to some only in music, but the Latin phrase comes
> nearest defining. The physical sensation – an outgoing of the mind.
> Augustine's prose has the dissolving irradiating power of music.
> Violin strings of his seem to crash into polemic discord and
> vituperation, or disquisition as subtle and in one sense as conceited as
> Donne, nearer him than any other soul.

Helen seems never to have made a straightforward translation from any
of St Augustine's works, but in a letter of rare self-revelation to her sister
she wrote:

> I suppose that phrase, 'Broken cisterns that can hold no water' and St
> Augustine's 'Thou hast made us for thyself, and our heart is restless
> till it finds rest in thee' are almost the deepest stains in the blotting
> paper which is my mind. I don't believe it was ever fear that moved
> me. It was a kind of homesickness – what some French writers call
> the *nostalgie de l'infini*.

Before going further, it may be well to outline the background to this
European medieval scholar born in Japan and brought up in Belfast
against the backcloth of her heredity. On a loose sheet of paper that gives
no indication of its purpose, she has sketched her ancestry in her own
inimitable fashion:

The original 'Grandfather William' of the family fought for the Covenant at Bothwell Brig in 1679, but escaped with his life; rode peaceably home, and when Claverhouse's dragoons came riding across the moors to take him a few days later, he baffled them by a trick that had more of Ulysses in it than of martyrdom: for the family tradition goes that he met them at his hall door with a courteous 'Gentlemen, you have ridden hard: you will be thirsty,' and had them in to a good meal and a better drink: and when the whole company was snoring drunk above and below the table, went out into the yard, cut the tethers of the horses and sent them galloping over the bogs, while himself and his sons rode down to the coast and took ship for Ireland. One of these sons made an excellent marriage, and got as his wife's dowry eight townlands near Newry in County Down, a mile or so from the house where Patrick Brontë, father of Charlotte and Emily and Anne, was born; only two townlands are left to them now, but some of the names are there to this day. My grandfather, Hugh Waddell, came from it to be minister in Glenarm, one of the Antrim glens: 'He was that well liked,' said an old woman to me, 'that if he had taken all that was offered him in one day in the Glens, he wouldn't ha' come home straight in the saddle.' He married Margaret, a sister of Captain Mayne Reid, author of *The Rifle Rangers* and *The Scalp Hunters* – I sat beside a man in the Paris Metro who was reading *The Rifle Rangers* in French, and they tell me he is very popular in Russia .... He was trapping on the Red River and the Missouri at twenty, held a commission in the American army, came back to Europe, settled down to novel-writing in London, made a fortune, and died a poor man. My father, his nephew, had his recklessness, tempered with a sanctity that was almost medieval; he went out as a pioneer missionary to Manchuria, and though the harshness of the climate drove him to a milder sky in Japan, he had a vast admiration for the Chinese till the day of his death, and was something of a sinologue, the Vicar of Wakefield turned Chinese scholar. He was profoundly, if absent-mindedly attached to his family, and after each furlough he brought back with him to Japan as many of us as he could afford. It was the habit of our youth – the two brothers and two sisters who made up the tail of a family of ten – to discuss endlessly how many times each of us had been round the world. I, the least of them, cut a poor figure in these global calculations, with only one and a half to my credit: and as the first voyage was at the unobservant age of one, my elders refused to count it. The last journey home was in the autumn of 1900, when my father was sixty and I eleven. In six months he was dead, with his manuscript, *The Interpretation of the Trinity to the Chinese Mind*, a mass of indecipherable notes, most of them in Chinese.

It had been an enchanted childhood: four of us behind the great bamboo fence that shut in a landscape garden with mountains and a pond and a stone bridge and a lizard that George trained to go up one sleeve and across his back and down the other. But looking back, the creative memory to me is the murmur of my father's voice, he pacing up and down the verandah in the early light and the household still asleep; the Psalms in Hebrew, the New Testament in Greek, the Lord's Prayer in Japanese. I still have his backless one-volume Shakespeare, underlined and annotated for the discriminating uses of 'soul' and 'spirit' and 'mind'.

There is nothing ostensibly autobiographical about any of Helen Waddell's published writings. When a BBC official asked her to spice a talk with incidents drawn from her own life, her uncompromising reaction was 'Damned if I will!' She never spoke of what lay closest to her heart; even intimate friends never guessed how she hoarded in her memory that enchanted childhood in Japan – it was shared only with her sister Meg. When at twelve years of age she returned with her family to Ireland and death claimed the father she worshipped, she secretly underwent a crisis of religious faith, decided that the goodness of God was a myth, rose in revolt against a savage, Puritan interpretation of life in terms solely of conscience and will, but was happily rescued from her state of despair when she chanced upon a copy of St Augustine's *Confessions* and met 'the living and victorious splendours' of medieval Latin verse in a little book on the library shelf of Ballygowan House. Concealing her own identity behind that of Ballygowan, the hospitable home of her great-aunt and uncle, the future medieval scholar wrote in an essay *Religio Loci* to be published in *The Manchester Guardian*:

> . . . At last it had found the passion for which it craved set beyond profanation in an unfamiliar tongue. If it was translated, it was as man believes in righteousness, with the heart. *Sero te amavi, pulchritudo tam antiqua, sero te amavi* – Late, late have I loved thee, O Beauty, so old and yet so new. *Rex tremendae majestatis* fell gratefully on ears that over-familiarity had often vexed: in *Quaerens me sedisti lassus*, it found passion enough to bankrupt whole anthologies.

Upon her return to school at Victoria College, Belfast, the twelve-year-old rebel found sufficient faith to summon her courage to the sticking-place, break her walk home with Cathleen Nesbitt to enter a Catholic church, view the liturgy in progress with deep emotion, dip her hand in the holy water stoup in order to make a large sign of the cross, and laughingly cover over awe and reverence with a reference to the Lord God hurling a thunderbolt on her Protestant head for consorting with the scarlet woman.

There was nothing of the narrow parochial bigot about Helen Waddell. She possessed a spirituality and wisdom akin to inspiration and prophecy, a power to identify herself not only with the living on earth, but also with the everliving we call dead, who have entered 'into the abode where the eternal are'. This Irish wandering scholar of the twentieth century revisited the past in a way that set her apart from all other workers in the field: where they studied the products of a dead civilization, she saw only men and women, weak and sinful, but familiar with fear, suffering, love and sheer heroism. She made her own John of Salisbury's affirmation in his *Polycraticus* or *Stateman's Book*: 'The dearest fruit of literature is this, that every grievous gulf of space and time annulled, it brings a man face to face with his friends.' Two of Helen's must be singled out for special mention – Alcuin and John of Salisbury himself, both typical Englishmen. Alcuin sprung from the fields and rocks above Spurn Head in Yorkshire, was an eighth century G. K. Chesterton figure of great gusto, hearty laughter, healthy appetite, capable of deep affection and lasting friendship, with an overall aura of unmistakable holiness. Greatest of English clerical schoolmasters, biblical scholar and liturgist, musician of the first rank, the Emperor Charlemagne's right-hand man in his task of rebuilding a tottering Europe by restoring its spiritual, intellectual and moral standards, he was content to retire for the last eight years of his life to the Benedictine monastery of Tours where, gladly returning to his rostrum, he encouraged his copyists to perfect the minuscule script, famed as the model and begetter of modern Roman typefaces. The serenity with which he faced death in 804 pervades the poem (see p.183), especially in its Virgilian echo, 'Beside the shore of the sail-winged sea'.

To the twelfth-century academic Ciceronian scholar, John of Salisbury, who stood head and shoulders above his contemporaries, life was 'immense, mysterious, unutterable'. No one exercised a greater influence over Helen Waddell's thought than this man whom John

Henry Newman included in his Catalogue of English Saints, added as Note D to the *Apologia* of 1843: '1180 October 25 John of Salisbury, B. of Chartres.' In 1928 Helen contributed a masterly essay on him to the *Essays and Studies* of The English Association; she frequently expressed the hope of writing a full-scale biography, a hope dashed by war and illness. She loved his analysis of music and the human voice, his defence of literature and the written word, than which only one human activity is greater – prayer, when 'the heart great with love, conceives the vision of God in the mind, and draws his greatness down as though with human hands'.

On the human level her father was the supreme influence in Helen's life, but her circle of just men made perfect would be incomplete without two more names: James Porter (1753–98), her eighteenth-century kinsman, and Dr George Pritchard Taylor, for forty-two years, until his death in 1920, a Presbyterian missionary in India. To look at James Porter is, in a strange way, to find oneself looking into the face of Hugh Waddell, his descendant. There is the same intense religious thirst for justice, the same intellectual brilliance, the same Irish humour, the same spiritual serenity when facing peril and death. Porter, born in 1753 in County Donegal, licensed by the Presbytery of Bangor, called to Grey Abbey and ordained in 1787, became an ardent champion of the poor in a land labouring under religious and political oppression. The cry of the French Revolution resounded in Ireland as in the rest of Europe. Like some eighteenth-century Bernard Shaw, Porter lampooned the bloodthirsty unprincipled landlords of the ascendancy, wrote satirical ballads set to catchy tunes under the pseudonym 'Billy Bluff', and demanded freedom of conscience and worship as well as equality for 800,000 Northerners whom they insulted, reviled and persecuted. An implacable Lord Londonderry, ridiculed as Lord Mountmumble, vowed revenge and seized the opportunity offered in 1798 when open rebellion broke out. As a clergyman, James Porter had never joined any organization and had steered clear of treason, but, knowing his life to be in danger, he went into hiding in the fourteen-mile stretch of cliffs and caverns of the Mourne Mountains. They could not long conceal him in the face of a large reward for his capture. He was seized and sentenced to execution on gallows to be erected within sight of his manse and his church. There are several variants of the tragic injustice, but according to Helen Waddell's:

His wife dragged herself and her children (she had eight, including a child at the breast) to plead for him ... At the last, dumb with agony, she came out to meet her husband as the grim procession came down the road. It halted to let him speak to her. He looked at her smiling. 'So, dearest,' he said, 'I am to sleep at home tonight.' It is one of the immortal stories, savagery and treachery and pain flowering at the gallow's foot into high poetry.

Recent research has revealed that, after death, James Porter's body was taken by his parishioners into his own home, laid on a sofa, and the door closed, but one of his children crept in, saw him lying there, and remarked: 'Father is sleeping long today.' His body lies in the cemetery of Grey Abbey under a gravestone which reads: 'Sacred to the memory of Rev. James Porter, Dissenting Minister of Grey Abbey who departed this life July 2nd 1798. Aged 45 years.' His two elder sons, Alexander and James, after years spent in evading spies, made their way to the land of freedom in America. There they both studied law, were called to the Bar, and by their integrity and legal knowledge raised the State of Louisiana to the pitch of American jurisprudence that it holds to this day, one as a judge of the Supreme Court, the other as Attorney-General. In 1935, when Nicholas Murray Butler, President of Columbia University, conferred on Helen Waddell a D.Litt. America was in fact honouring a descendant of two of its most illustrious sons, for Alexander Porter was the only Irishman ever to represent Louisiana in the United States Senate, and more than once he refused nomination for the office of Governor. It is not then surprising that as Helen stood on board the SS Berengaria as it entered the harbour, she saw through the mist not skyscrapers but campaniles, a New York that was an island of ancient churches with high bell-towers:

> *The presence that so strangely rose beside the waters.*
> Torcello with its single campanile
> Above blackthorn and salt lagoon
> Multiplied in the mist.
> Island of stooping bell-towers, Holy Island ...
> Byzantium with Christ an emperor,
> Byzantium not any more a ghost.

History, as Helen Waddell was quick to realize in her study of the Middle Ages, is made up of men and women. Human life does not exist in a vacuum: past and present are for ever moving towards the goal of eternity. The twentieth century has witnessed unprecedented upheaval: like the tenth it has been a century of 'iron, lead and darkness' with very few streaks of gold. There is, however, a rhythm, a periodicity about the mystery of time that presages a sequent period of comparatively peaceful renewal such as nature itself demands. Are the supra-racial reformers, at present planning to take a united Europe into the twenty-first century, likely to confine their efforts to the establishment of an internationalism of political economists, or will they prove to be statesmen of vision, anxious to build a spiritual whole with a sense of historic and organic unity? Looking back over fourteen centuries of Benedictine monastic life, a cloistered nun wonders whether the time has come to produce an Ecumenical Menology of saintly men and women drawn from every religious tradition, for as John of Salisbury has well said, 'In every darkness, God hath his stars; in every religion he is the shepherd of faithful souls.' Were such a compilation to be made, then the final name to be included in the catalogue of those who penetrated Helen Waddell's life at a profound level – that of the Reverend George Pritchard Taylor MA, DD (1855–1920) – would merit consideration. Born in the Gujerat province of India, he graduated from Queen's University, Belfast, was ordained to the Presbyterian ministry, returned to India in 1877, founded and governed the Stevenson Memorial College of Ahmadabad, and spent the rest of his life there, returning to Europe only twice, in 1890 and 1914. In his missionary zeal, human tenderness, charity and humility he appears a very personification of St Francis de Sales (1567–1622), each ruled by the same dictum, 'The measure of love is to love without measure.' When Dr Taylor met Helen at her home in 1914, his keen intuition summed up her predicament very exactly: the selfish demanding stepmother, the lack of any independence, the intellectual frustration, the financial straits. With exquisite tact, he asked Helen to allow him to set aside a small sum to buy the books she needed. He was childless: the small sum gradually grew until he was satisfied at having made her future financially secure. During the First World War weekly letters between the two braved torpedo action and brought solace and love to them both. She became a 'dear daughter', and from addressing him as 'Dear' for a year or two Helen finally capitulated and admitted him to the sanctum hitherto reserved solely for her own father. Many letters to Dr Taylor will be found in the following pages: not one letter of his in its entirety is extant. During the last decade of her life, when Alzheimer's disease made its terrible inroads upon Helen's mind, she apparently took his letters and slashed out of each one any reference to herself. After his death Helen's letters were dispatched to her sister at Kilmacrew, and so escaped the later holocaust made at Primrose Hill Road, London.

In an early letter to Dr Taylor, Helen described her childhood in Tokyo. Every evening all came together and one of the group would read aloud to the listening family, leading off in the place of honour with a chapter from the King James' Bible of 1611, read from first page to last once a year, and committed in chunks to memory. Helen's bible, a stout little volume 7½ × 4 × 2½ inches thick, bound between wooden boards prettily ornamented in scarlet and green with an incised design on bevelled edges, has furnished the scriptural caption to each passage included in this selection. Only once is a verse – that of 1 John 4 – firmly underlined: 'Ye are of God, little children, . . . greater is he that is in you, than he that is in the world.' The gift of a decorated bible to his little eight-year-old daughter Helen, who had delighted her father's heart by committing to memory the Letter to the Hebrews from the opening verse of chapter 1 to the 25th verse of chapter 13, strongly suggests that he was providing her with a principle to act on for the rest of her life. This anthology, drawn from Helen Waddell's writings, is concerned mainly with the shape of the Christian life; it is not perhaps without significance that the assembled material seemed to fall naturally within the context of divine revelation. Hugh Waddell's child was worthy of her father.

In retrospect, Helen Waddell's life of seventy-five years may be divided into three sections. Firstly, there were the years of bitter negation: at three years of age, Helen lost her mother, and at twelve, her father. Following her undergraduate days, she spent ten years, sacrificing her youth in silent endurance, bereft of companionship and intellectual stimulation, subject night and day to the whims of a carping alcoholic stepmother whose death in 1920 set her free at last to go up to Oxford.

Then came the years of enrichment and fulfilment preceding the outbreak of the Second World War, years that saw the publication and wide acclaim of all her major works. She travelled, studied for two years in Paris, settled finally in London, made a host of friends, breakfasted with Stanley Baldwin, lunched at Her Majesty's special invitation with Queen Mary at 10 Downing Street, organized a 'Ministry of All Talents' that included celebrities such as Bernard Shaw, Max Beerbohm, Walter de la Mare, Rose Macaulay and Margot Asquith, all of them dazzled by the smiling modesty of this small medieval scholar with her seductive Irish brogue, salt wit, and feminine charm.

Finally, there were the years, unfinished and undone, spent in breaking her will upon the will of God. Possibly a too-close identification during the War with her beloved Japanese, mutilated or annihilated by the atom bomb, had a devastating effect on Helen's mind and nervous system, and led to total collapse, causing her to fall an easy prey to the inexorable advance of Alzheimer's disease. She was to pass the last decade of her life as a graduate in what Peter of Celles, John of Salisbury's friend, called 'the school of the simplicity of Christ'. The ineradicable image left in the mind is not that of the scholar who brought the Middle Ages to life, but that of a Christian of deep humility and compassion seated in surrender before a picture of Christ her master stumbling up the hill of Calvary. With tears in her eyes, she said to Nichole Vaudremer, who had known her in Paris in days long past, 'My cross is very heavy too but, looking at him, I try to carry it without being too complaining and sorry for myself.' One can but imagine the anguish of Meg, that sister of whom Helen had once written: 'We were like a tree that forked so near the root it looked like two trees, but in the earth there's only one.' A poignant entry in the diary Meg kept of those last years reads: 'God help her. What has brought her to this?' To which Helen would have made reply: 'One comes back to the wisdom of the Middle Ages: *mors janua vitae* – death the gate of life. We believed in the life everlasting, but into the life everlasting we have come to read the life eternal, life infinite in its breadth and length and depth and height. For to know the will of God was not Paul's ultimate seeking. It began 'with the knowledge of his will'; it ended 'with all the fullness of God'.

On 5 March 1965 Helen Jane Waddell left behind the unsubstantial shadow of time to enter upon that eternity that had ever besieged her life.

> Thou hast the freedom of heaven: and now to thee
> The glories kept for virgin souls are given.
> Upon thy radiant head a glittering crown,
> And in thy hand the joyous green of the palm.

> John Milton: *Lament for Damon*

Part One

THE BEGINNING
AND
THE END

'I am Alpha and Omega, the
beginning and the ending, saith the
Lord, which is, and which was,
and which is to come, the Almighty.'

Rev. 1.8

1 I AM
(Exod. 3.14)

BERNARD SYLVESTRIS OF TOURS

This *Nous* is the intellect of God, God the supreme, powerful beyond all power, its nature born of his divinity. There are the types of all things living, the eternal ideas, the intelligible world, the knowledge of things that are to be: there, as in a clear mirror may one see the generations, the mysterious destiny of the creation of God. There, in kind, in species, in very idiosyncrasy, are written those things which the first Chaos, which the world, which the elements themselves shall bring to birth. There, graven by the finger of the supreme Accountant, the texture of time, the foredoomed consequence, the disposition of the centuries. There are the tears of the poor and the fortunes of kings: there the soldier's pomp, and the happier discipline of the philosopher: there, whatever the reason of angels or men may comprehend: there whatever heaven holds in its wide arches. And since these things are so, not disparate is it from eternity, nor separate from the nature and substance of God.

BOETHIUS

And in the midst the Maker sits on high:
The reins are in his hands,
Master and King, the well-spring and the source,
The Law and arbiter of equity.

More Latin Lyrics

Lord, Thy eternity dost ever besiege our life. Thou dost never depart from us, and we hardly return to Thee. All our life Thou has sought us: seek us still. By the mystery of Thy holy Incarnation, by Thy Cross and Passion, by Thy glorious Resurrection, speak to us yet. We ask it for the sake of that Life which Thou didst give for the life of the world. Amen.

Unpublished typescript

2 THE FIRST AND THE LAST
(*Rev. 22.13*)

HILDEBERT

Alpha and Omega, God, my God!
All-wise, Almighty and all-good
Fount of goodness, Eloi,
Summum Bonum, God most High!
Over, under all, Thou art:
All within, from all a part:
From without dost all enfold,
From beneath dost all uphold:
Over all things dost preside,
Immanent in all abide.
Thou in all dost all transcend:
All from Thee, their All, depend.
Within, without, above, below,
Thou art all, yet all not Thou:
Thou unmoved art motion's cause,
Changeless giv'st to change its laws:
Time and space obey Thy word:
Thou their timeless spaceless Lord.
From necessity's decree
Lives Thy sovrain Being free.
Our tomorrow yesteryear
Unto Thee are now and here:
Future, present, past are all
One today perpetual:
All things momently foreseeing
Thou dost bring to perfect being,
Fashioned out of chaos blind
To the pattern of Thy mind.
All my hope in Thee I place,
All I ask, God, is Thy grace.

More Latin Lyrics

3 SON OF THE FATHER
(*2 John 3*)

THOMAS AQUINAS

The Word went forth,
  Yet from his Father never went away.
Came to his work on earth,
And laboured till the twilight of his day.

Men envied him: He went to death,
By his own man betrayed,
Yet first to his own men himself had given
In wine and broken bread.

In birth he gave himself a friend to men,
At meat, their holy bread:
Dying, he gave himself their ransoming:
Reigning, their high reward.

O Victim slain for us and our salvation,
Opening the doors of light,
The warring hosts are set on our damnation,
Give us the strength to fight.

More Latin Lyrics

4 I WILL POUR OUT MY SPIRIT
(*Joel 2.28*)

HILDEBERT

O Holy Ghost, O faithful Paraclete,
  Love of the Father and the Son.
In whom Begetter and Begotten meet ...
Bond that holdeth God to man.

17

Power that welds in one
Humanity and Deity.
God making all that is
Before our day.
God guiding all that's made
Throughout our day,
Gift that abides through an eternity
Of giving, and is made no less.
Thy going forth preceded Time,
Thy pouring forth took place in Time.
The one, the well spring of power and the river of grace,
The other, the flowing, the giving, the light on our face.
Thou camest forth from thy transcendent day,
To make for us this shining feasting day.
Thou who alone
Art worthily adored
With Father and with Son.
To Thee in heart and word
Be honour, worship, grace,
Here and in every place,
World without end. Amen.

More Latin Lyrics

5 TO HIM BE GLORY AND DOMINION

(*1 Pet. 5.11*)

Do not give up the sermons in little. You've chosen one of my own 'elect' in that verse from 2 Peter, 'partakers of the divine nature'. And do not give up that idea of God as the 'Eternal Now', for it seems to me His infinity and eternity are little stressed: and they explain so much. Has anybody ever preached on the clause, 'One day is with the Lord as a thousand years, and a thousand years as one day'? For that first clause seems to me to suggest the true infinity, more than the speed of the second. The first makes a man's life short enough, but as deep as a thousand years: in the second, the whole world's life is just a scattering of raindrops.

On Friday I went to sit and deliberate with the Committee of the Girls' Auxiliary. They had a good many prayers for public occasions – it was Ezekiel's vision: behold they were very dry. And then I saw. The one for Bible Circle is almost ready: 'O Bread of God that camest down from heaven to give life unto the world: give us to know that the written word is as the veil which was thy flesh, and hid thy glory from all but the desiring heart. Grant that in handling it we may indeed lay hold on that eternal life which was with the Father, and is tabernacled with men.'

There was another that I hadn't the courage to send. You may have it:

'Father, we thank Thee for our happiness: for Thy great gift of life: for the wonder and bloom of the world. We bless Thee that it takes a very little thing to make us happy, yet so great a thing to satisfy us that only Thyself canst do it, for Thou alone art greater than our hearts. We bless Thee for Thy calling which is so high that no man can perfectly attain unto it, and for Thy grace which stoops so low that none of us can ever fall too low for it. Above all we bless Thee that Thou didst send Thy Son, Jesus Christ our Lord, for having seen Him we have seen Thee, whose truth doth ever warm, and whose grace doth ever keep. Amen.

To Dr Taylor, 17 November 1917

6 GOD IS GREATER THAN OUR HEART
(*1 John 3.20*)

I'm copying out for you a scrap from George Adam Smith on Isaiah that bears upon a theory of mine. 'He said, Surely they are my people, children that will not lie; so He was their Saviour. The "surely" is not the *fiat* of sovereignty or of foreknowledge: it is the hope and confidence of love. It did not prevail: it was disappointed.'

This is, of course, a profound acknowledgement of men's free-will. It is implied that men's conduct must remain an uncertain thing, and that in calling men, God cannot adventure upon greater certainty than is implied in the trust of affection. If one asks, 'What, then, about God's foreknowledge, who alone knoweth the end of a thing from the beginning, and his sovereign grace, who chooseth whom He will – are you not logically bound to these?' then it can only be asked in return – 'Is it not better to be without logic for a little if, at the expense of it, we obtain so true, so deep a glimpse into God's heart as this simple verse affords us?' Which is better for us to know — that God is Wisdom which knows all, or Love that dares and ventures all? Surely, that God is Love which dares and ventures all, with the worst, with the most hopeless of us. This is what makes this single verse of Scripture more powerful to move the heart than all creeds or catechisms. For where these speak of sovereign will, and often mock our affections with the bare and heavy (if legitimate) sceptre that they sway, this calls forth our love, honour, and obedience by the heart it betrays in God. Of what unsuspicious trust, of what chivalrous adventure of love, of what fatherly confidence does it speak! What a religion is this of ours in the power of which a man may every morning rise and feel himself thrilled by the thought that God trusts him enough to work with His will for the day: in the power of which a man may look round and see a sordid, hopeless human life glorified by the truth, that for the salvation of such God did *adventure* Himself in a love that laid itself down in death.

Unspecified autograph

7 BEHOLD, IT WAS VERY GOOD
(*Gen. 1.31*)

From the cathedral at the further end a low oddly resonant voice was speaking, half chanting. Broceliande, he was saying, and the woods of the Ardennes, and Italian Silo that sees from its high pines the white sails of twin seas. What kind of wizard was the little man, that when he spoke you saw what he saw, yet on those white sails neither your eyes nor his had ever rested. It was rivers now, the waters of Shiloh that go softly, the Tiber that bears Rome upon his shoulders, the Po that rolls towards Venice its imperious way. And now it was the stars. This must be the poem of which Hildebert had spoken – the making of the world from chaos and old night: and still the little figure swung there, gazing out under a penthouse of great brows and a thatch of black hair, his short-sighted eyes rapt and unaware, unless of the vision within. He had halted. The rhythm changed into prose, yet if anything more resonant than his verse:

> Perfect from the perfect, beautiful from the beautiful, eternal from the eternal: from the intellectual world the sensible world was born: full was that which bore it, and its plenitude fashioned it full.

Since John Scotus Erigena, said Abelard to himself, there has been no philosopher who was a poet also: and he began remembering the close of Erigena's *De Divisione Naturae*, his prayer for the coming of Light that will bring to darkness the false light of the philosophers, and will lighten the darkness of those that know. The memory had carried him into a soundless place, and how long he had been deaf he did not know...

> A land there is, a little lap of earth,
> Near neighbour to the dawn and the south wind,
> The first to feel the sweet new-risen sun,
> Nor hurt at all by his primaeval fire.
> It knoweth but the clemency of heaven,
> And in one lap holds the delights of earth.
> Amid those happy woods a river flows
> That winds and turns again upon itself,
> Chiding the roots and warring with the pebbles,
> Till with a murmuring of fleeting water
> It falls into the level of the lake.
> Here to these water-meadows, flowering fair,
> Came man, a while their guest: too brief a guest.

'Too brief a guest,' he repeated.

Peter Abelard

8 UPSIDE DOWN
(*Isa. 29.16*)

Too brief a guest. But shall the clay say to him that fashioneth it, 'What makest thou?' Shall the thing framed say of him that framed it, 'He had no understanding?' 'Yea. The soul cries out upon the body: and I have heard the body cry out upon the soul, to the Creator of them both. "Daily the soul complains of me", it cried, because I conform to my own nature and dishonour her daily. But thou didst fashion me of earth: how can I but smell of it? Had I been fashioned of things clean, then might she blame me for my filthiness. Now, rather might she cry out on that which made me of such stuff, and yoked us in one yoke.' Aye, and I have seen the souls of the unborn, huddled by the house of Cancer the Crab, and pure in their simple essence, they shudder at the dull and blind habitations which they see prepared.

Dull and blind. So dull? So blind? I tell you, let the spirit complain of the flesh no more. It is the prison which makes men free. I tell you, this flesh is the condition of their immortality. For in mastering it does the mortal become immortal, and humanity pass to the proud gods. Let you but look at a man's eyes! The beasts run downcast, looking at the earth, but the very face of man is witness to his majesty: alone on earth he rears his sacred head to the stars. The Gods themselves, and the sky, and the stars, hold speech with him: he is one with the council of the Fates, aye, and by that same base act of generation, throws the gauntlet down to Atropos. He shall bring to light the dark causes of things, lost in the mirk; he shall see the windy fields of the air, he shall see the dark silence of the dead. His is the height of heaven, and the breadth of the earth, and the depths of the sea, and he shall know the changing face of things, and why they change. He shall subdue the earth and rule upon it, the first of things created, their king and their high priest.

But the stains: but love, *tyrannus amor*, the tyrant of our flesh: but the whole ineradicable evil of the ancient wood? So be it. Earth to earth: but be thou heaven's familiar, and let your eyes depart not from those high places. For when this house falls in ruin about thee, they shall abide thy coming, familiar roofs of home. No unkind stranger shalt thou climb there, where waits thee the place and the banner of thy star.

Peter Abelard

9 MY GOD, MY STRENGTH
(*Ps. 18.2*)

BEDE

O God that art the only hope of the world,
The only refuge for unhappy men,
Abiding in the faithfulness of heaven,
Give me strong succour in this testing place.
O King, protect thy man from utter ruin
Lest the weak faith surrender to the tyrant,
Facing innumerable blows alone.
Remember I am dust, and wind, and shadow,
And life as fleeting as the flower of grass.
But may the eternal mercy which hath shone
From time of old
Rescue thy servant from the jaws of the lion.
Thou who didst come from on high in the cloak of flesh,
Strike down the dragon with that two-edged sword
Whereby our mortal flesh can war with the winds
And beat down strongholds, with our Captain God.

There are cadences in his prose lovelier than anything in his poetry –
'Burn now your candle as long as ye will: it has naught to do with me, for
my light cometh when the day breaketh.' But the poet is in the strange
burst of weeping that took him under a tree in the open, in a line or two
of his vision of hell –

> Where there is no voice unless of bitter weeping,
> No face, unless the face of the tormentors.

and the wistful beauty of his heaven –

> Nor any night
> To snatch the splendour of the gracious light:
> Nor sorrow comes, nor tears, nor tired old age.

More Latin Lyrics

23

10 GOD SAID, LET US MAKE MAN
(*Gen. 1.26*)

When in his *De Mundi Universitate,* Bernard Sylvestris comes to the making of man in that place of green woods and falling streams he holds, plainly and determinedly, the dignity of his creation. He has his discrimination among the senses: in his glory of sight he is in the tradition that begins with Augustine's 'O queen light, sovereign of the senses'; of the others, he speaks generously yet without that transport. Of generation itself, plainly and fearlessly, the Greek ideal of moderation, of discretion: and then the poet sees in the very physical act the eternal war between life and death, the reweaving of the thread that has been snapped by Atropos' shears. Only, he would have a man fix his eye upon the stars and, his term ended, thither let him go: *hospes haud incognita,* a guest not unknown.

'Perfect from the perfect, beautiful from the beautiful, eternal from the eternal: from the intellectual world the sensible world was born: full was that which bore it, and its plenitude fashioned it full.' The war between the spirit and the flesh has ended in a Truce of God, even as the Last Judgement of the Western rose-window in Chartres melts into 'heaven's own colour, blue'. St Bernard of Clairvaux spoke of the dungheap of the flesh: Bernard Sylvestris saw in their strange union a discipline that made for greatness, and the body itself a not ignoble hospice for the pilgrim soul. The spirit is richer for its limitations; this is the prison that makes men free. His Adam is the Summer of Chartres Cathedral, naked, fearless, and unbowed. He saw him as Michael Angelo did, wistful, beautiful, potent for evil or for good, already prescient of the travail that God hath given to the sons of men that they may be exercised in it. 'He hath made everything beautiful in his time,' continues the voice of Ecclesiastes which John of Salisbury found so strangely poignant. 'Also He hath set the world in their heart, so that no man can find out the work that God maketh from the beginning to the end.' And if the world of Bernard Sylvestris is a dewdrop too crystalline for philosophy or experience, it is for that moment of vision that poets are born.

The Wandering Scholars

11 BORN OF GOD
(*John 1.13*)

BOETHIUS

There is no race of men
But rose from one same spring.
One Father of them all,
To all things giving.
He gave the sun his beams
The moon her crescent of light,
To earth he gave mankind,
Stars to the night.
Prisoner in body, soul
Besieged by heaven,
Mortality is sprung
From a noble stock.

Why bluster about race,
And brag of ancestry?
If you would look at that from whence you came,
God that begot you,
Not one
Would prove a degenerate son
Or cling
To the evil thing,
Lest he should lose his way
To his primeval spring.

More Latin Lyrics

12 PONDER THE PATH OF THY FEET
(*Prov. 4.26*)

COLUMBANUS

O Life, how greatly thou hast cheated, how many thou hast blinded, how many led astray. Thou fliest, and art nothing: seen, thou art a shadow: in stay, a wreath of smoke that daily vanishes and daily comes again: in coming, thou fliest, in flying, comest: unlike in thy event, alike in thy beginning: unlike in thy bestowing, alike in thy passing: to fools a sweetness, bitter to the wise. Yet thou hadst been true, if the sin of the first transgression had not broken thee, left thee tottering and mortal. A road to life art thou, not Life.... And there is no man makes his dwelling in the road, but walks there: and those who fare along the road have their dwelling in the fatherland. So thou art that naught, O mortal life, naught but a road, a fleeting ghost, an emptiness, a cloud uncertain and frail, a shadow and a dream.

More Latin Lyrics

Part Two

IMAGE OF
THE INVISIBLE
GOD

'Giving thanks unto the Father . . . .
Who hath delivered us from the
power of darkness, and hath
translated us into the kingdom of
his dear Son. . . . Who is the
image of the invisible God, the
firstborn of every creature.'

Col. 1.12–15

13 THE ROOT OF DAVID
(*Rev. 22.16*)

It was like the old story, Jacob thought: here was a young girl coming to the well, just as his mother had come long before he was born; and here was himself come all those leagues to meet her. Was it to meet her? Was this the woman who was to be his wife?

She had come nearer. He could see how young she was and how slender. Jacob turned to the herdsmen: 'Why don't you water the sheep?' 'We wait till someone rolls away the stone,' they said placidly, 'it is a heavy stone.' Jacob turned his back on them, set his teeth and tugged; the stone went back with a great heave, and he turned to find Rachel gazing at him. Then Jacob did the suddenest thing he had ever done in his life; he stooped and kissed her. And then he did what surprised himself even more – he cried. He was sick with loneliness. He pulled himself together, told Rachel who he was, they began watering the sheep together, and then Rachel ran home to tell her father. Laban came out to meet him, and made a great fuss of him, and brought him home.

Jacob sat trying to attend to his uncle's questions, and wondering when Rachel would lift her head and look at him. Jacob had thought he was hungry, but he was too excited to eat. He had thought he was tired out, but when he went to bed he was too eager to sleep. His mind would do nothing but go over and over all the few things she had said to him, and how she had looked when she said them. For the first time in his life Jacob had found that it was possible to care for someone else more than for himself.

Stories from Holy Writ

> I went out at the Eastern Gate,
> I saw the girls in clouds,
> Like clouds they were, and soft and bright,
> But in the crowds
> I thought on the maid who is my light,
> Down-drooping, soft as the grey twilight;
> She is my mate.

Lyrics from the Chinese

14 RACHEL CALLED HER SON JOSEPH
(*Gen. 30.24*)

I sympathized with Saintsbury for a brief moment on Friday. I went down to the service on the anniversary of the outbreak of war. Dr McDermot spoke admirably, but he read his text from the Revised Version: 'The Lord, the Almighty, reigneth.' And one's memory thundered back at him, 'The Lord God Omnipotent reigneth.'

I was writing yesterday the October article for *Daybreak* — the seven years serving. And for the first time 'it was revealed to me' that there was a greatness in Jacob, apart even from that strange second sight of the spirit which seems almost arbitrary. It will be so long before you see it in print that I want to quote bits of it to you now: it's after the offer to Laban of himself for seven years, when Laban rose up and went contentedly to bed, and Jacob went out under the stars, for the wild happiness would not let him sleep. 'He had done a mad thing: for seven years he had sold himself, made himself a slave with not so much as would buy him fresh sandals when these wore out: but it was the wisest and the greatest thing he had ever done. All his life Jacob had taken all that he could, and given not at all: now for the first time he gave, and gave greatly: himself, for seven years of his youth. On those same Mesopotamian plains Satan had answered God, sneering — "Skin for skin, yea, all that a man hath will he give for his life." But Jacob's heart was crying "Life for life, yea, all that a man hath will he give for love."'

And it is not only the original gift: it was the love of the imagination that Francis Thompson thinks is of late days only that transfigures him — and transfigured those seven years. He was a cheat and a supplanter, and yet

> By the vision splendid
> Was on his way attended.

I am glad I have seen it. It makes so much more intelligible that hard saying, 'Jacob have I loved, and Esau hated.'

To Dr Taylor, 8 August 1916

15 A NEW COMMANDMENT I GIVE UNTO YOU
(John 13.34)

Francis Thompson's essay on Shelley was brought out at the same time as *The Hound of Heaven*: Meynell calls them twins. Certainly the Shelley essay burst on me as a most wonderful surprise, and I felt almost intoxicated by the exuberant wealth and beauty of its diction. I don't remember ever reading anything that for the time just swept me off my feet so completely. His phrasing seems to me almost *ne plus ultra* of melodiously-woven sentences, the exquisite expression of thoughts themselves most exquisite. His paper on 'Paganism Old and New' is a striking and eloquent affirmation of the beauty proper to Christian literature. May I quote:

> The distance between Catullus and the *Vita Nuova*, between Ovid and the *House of Life*, can be measured only by Christianity. The lover of poetry owes a double gratitude to his Creator Who, not content with giving us salvation on the Cross, gave us also, at the marriage of Cana in Galilee, Love. For there Love was consecrated, and declared the child of Jehovah, not of Jove; there virtually was inaugurated the whole successive order of those love-poets who have shown the world that passion, in putting on chastity, put on also tenfold beauty. For purity is the sum of all loveliness, as whiteness is the sum of all colours.

In his essay on Shelley he had referred to that poet's presentment of 'Free love in its most odious form' as one of but three passages to which exception can be taken regarding the purity of Shelley's poetry. But here is to me an astonishing note appended to 'Paganism Old and New'. Having stated in the text, 'Body differs not more from soul than the Amor of Catullus or Ovid differs from the love of Dante or Shelley', he adds as a footnote on Shelley: 'An anti-Christian in ethics, but the blood in the veins of his Muse was Christian. The spirit of his treatment of love is – with few, if any, exceptions – entirely Christian.'

Can this be true? I hope so, if only that we may revise our, shall I say ecclesiastical? estimate of that 'enchanted child' who, its brief life through, was 'worn by warfare with itself, its Maker, and all the world'. By the way, did you know that 'the supreme Italian poet and the supreme English poet bore almost an identical surname'? Thompson in his essay on Dante affirms this to be the case. It seems Alighiero is probably derived from the German Aldinger, and means 'Rule-spear'. And listen to this on Milton: 'Milton found his daughters undutiful. Poor little undutiful daughters. Fathers had terrible conceptions of duties in those days. Did any one ever want to know Milton? Did any one ever not want to know Shakespeare?'

To Dr Taylor, May 1916

16 THEY SOLD JOSEPH FOR TWENTY PIECES OF SILVER
(*Gen. 37.28*)

This is a story that ends in Egypt, but it does not begin there. It begins more than a hundred years before Moses was found in the bulrushes: and it began with an old oak tree at Hebron in Palestine and in a big black tent.

[The tree we had was a beech, but it doesn't matter: it was on a mound in the Moss Field, with short dry grass, and the wind always blows there, just as it used to blow on Abraham's face when he came to sit at his tent door in the evening and watch the sun going down. And our tent was only a big black umbrella, but it covered us all if we sat very tight.]

It was an old tent, for first of all Abraham had lived here, and then his son Isaac, and now it was Isaac's son Jacob. Jacob had been in foreign parts nearly all his life, but when he was old he came back to the old oak and the old tent, and settled down. But there was a crowd of little tents round it now, for he had twelve sons, and herds and herds of cows and sheep and goats. But at the time this story begins it was very quiet in the big black tent, for ten of the older ones were away, and the only two at home were Joseph and a very little one called Benjamin. Joseph was the son that his father liked best, except of course for Benjamin: but then everyone loved Benjamin, he was so fat and so small, tumbling about like a puppy. Even the big brothers, who were a very tough lot, liked

32

Benjamin. But they hated Joseph; he was their stepbrother, and his father's favourite, and they jeered at him for his good manners and his pride and his queer, dreamy ways.

Stories from Holy Writ

17 SHARP IRON
(*Prov. 27.17*)

I came on such a fascinating suggestion about Tarsus, about the harbour having once borne Cleopatra's fleet, I harked back to *Antony and Cleopatra*, and found that gorgeous description of Cleopatra sailing down the Cydnus:

> The barge she sat in like a burnished throne
> Burned on the water . . .

Well, it was to meet Mark Antony at Tarsus, about forty years before Paul was born. And Antony's subjugation is the great metaphor for the subjugation of Rome by the East – by the Greek civilization too, for Cleopatra was pure Greek, as well as 'gypsy'. It's *only* a metaphor, but it is a perfect jumping-off place for an impression of the *ensemble* that Paul was born into.

This, being the last Sunday of April, was the Sacrament. I like that old word far better than Communion. After it was over, and we came out into the sunlight and the crowds, the contrast after the silence was almost dizzy. We were the last to come out, and just as we came down the steps, the organ was playing in the empty church; somehow it seems to me that this ending with music is one of the loveliest things in a service, for the sound came after us, almost wistfully, like an appeal of things sacred to have some sway over an alien life, the last cast of the net of the 'sanctuary'. That's a word I love, especially with the mediaeval association. Tell me, don't you love the Latin hymns of the Middle Ages? The first time I read *Uncle Tom's Cabin* –I must have been about nine – the clearest memory I have of it is the 'veneration' that came on me when I came to the three lines quoted from the *Dies Irae*:

> Recordare, Jesu pie. . . .

It was partly sheer reverence for Latin, which I don't believe I ever lost, and partly because there is enchantment in the very words. Do you remember, 'Quaerens me sedisti lassus'? There is one incomparable line in the English rendering:

> Seeking me Thy worn feet hasted.

As for the glorious descant of *Jerusalem the Golden* in Latin or English, it seems to satisfy the natural soul of beauty in the church as nothing else can do.

Dear, I must go and see about Joseph. I am crushed to think of his lone patience. Even after the chief butler went back to high estate — two years — 'two full years' it says. The Book of Genesis is an extraordinarily detached piece of work, but here and there you get a sudden sympathetic suggestion like that. I've been looking up the psalm about him: it says there, 'until the word of the Lord tried him'. I did not know it was said of him, 'the iron entered into his soul'. At any rate, it didn't poison it.

To Dr Taylor, 25 April 1915

18 THE LORD SHOWED HIM MERCY
(*Gen. 39.21*)

It was sunset; and Joseph went out from the presence of the Captain of the Guard, bound, between two soldiers. He was going to the King's Prison. And that night, in the black dark of the dungeon, with chains on his hands and heavy fetters on his feet, there came a terrible darkness on his soul.

Joseph never forgot that night in prison. Long after, someone wrote a psalm about him, and told how they 'afflicted his feet with fetters', put heavy chains upon him; and then — it is one of the strangest lines ever written — 'the iron entered into his soul'. It is not so hard a thing to have iron on one's flesh. Thousands of years after, Paul and Silas lay in a dungeon at Philippi, and they cared so little about their chains that they were singing. But then they felt that the Lord Christ was with them; while Joseph — it seemed to him that God had forgotten him. He had gone away and left him, and there was no one to care for his soul. It did

34

not matter whether you tried to be good or not. God did not care. The beautiful woman who had tempted him was safe and petted and cared for, fast asleep now and happy; and he was out in the dark, chained like a dog. He had been a fool to think God cared what you did. He did not care any more than if you were a fly buzzing on a windowpane. He did not care what happened to you. He was cruel. The chains had come very near Joseph's soul.

And then something happened. I wonder if you remember a story about a prison, long after, where Peter lay asleep, chained between two soldiers; how an angel came and touched the chains, and they fell off, and he stood up free. That is what happened here. Joseph saw no angel, and the chains did not fall off his hands. But God Himself came and touched the crueller chains that were hurting his soul, and they dropped, and it was his soul that stood up free. The man who told the story in Hebrew long ago does not say very much about it; he only says, 'The Lord shewed him kindness'. But God's kindness is so wonderful a thing that if a man once gets a sight of it he never can forget. He did not tell Joseph why this cruel thing had happened to him. He did not even say that He would make it up to him. He only made him feel that He was there, that He had not forgotten, and Joseph's heart went out to Him in a great adoration. He did not care any more what chains were upon him, so long as he was God's.

We know now why it was, though Joseph did not. It was to make him fit to be overseer, not of the greatest house in Egypt, but of all Egypt itself. But it was years before Joseph knew; and the years were long years.

Stories from Holy Writ

19 BE RECONCILED TO THY BROTHER
(Matt. 5.24)

Joseph looked at his brothers in silence. At last he spoke. 'Come near to me,' he said, and held out his hands to them, and they came slowly near. 'I am Joseph, your brother,' he said, speaking very slowly, that they might take it in, 'whom ye sold into Egypt. But you are not to be grieved or angry with yourselves, for God sent me before you to preserve life. For these two years hath the famine been in the land: and there are still five years to come, in which there shall be neither ploughing nor harvest. And God sent me before you to save your lives by a great deliverance. So, now,' he almost coaxed them, 'it was not you who sent me here, but God; and He has made me a father to Pharaoh, and lord of his house, and ruler of all Egypt. And now, make haste and go to my father and say to him, "*Thy son, Joseph, says; God hath made me lord of all Egypt; come down unto me, and thou shalt dwell in the land of Goshen, and shalt live near me, thou and thy children and grandchildren, and all thy flocks and thy herds, and I will feed thee.*" You see with your own eyes, and my brother Benjamin sees, that it is I who speak to you. And tell my father of all my glory in Egypt, and of all that ye have seen; and ye must haste and bring my father here.'

And then he turned and held out his arms to Benjamin, and one by one his brothers came up and he kissed them every one, and after that, it says, they all talked with him.

And so the story goes back to where it began, with an old man sitting at the door of the big black tent, in Hebron, and watching for his sons; and it tells how they came with a great caravan, and how they told the wonderful news, and the old man's heart fainted. He could not believe them. Again and again they told him what Joseph had said, but still he shook his head, and then Judah took his arm and said, 'Come and see the fine carriage he sent to bring you to him,' and his spirit revived. 'It is enough,' he said, 'Joseph my son, is yet alive; I will go and see him before I die.' And the story ends like that other story that our Lord Christ told, 'his father saw him, and ran, and fell on his neck and kissed him.'

It is a good story to end the year with, for it ends in a reconciling. And when you think of Joseph planning how to bring his brothers' hearts back, will you remember Someone greater than Joseph who devised means that His banished might not be expelled from Him. And when you think of Judah offering to suffer in his little brother's stead, will you remember Someone kinder than Judah who suffered for all His little brothers on the bitter cross. And it is a good story to begin the year with, for, after all, what one sees in it most is not so much the loving kindness of Joseph, as the loving kindness of God, God who redeemeth the souls of His servants.

Stories from Holy Writ

20 THE VIRGIN'S NAME WAS MARY
(*Luke 1.27*)

ANON. tenth century

The sadness of the wood is bright
With young green sprays, the apple trees
Are laden, in their nests high overhead
Wood pigeons croon.

The doves make moan, deep throated sings the thrush,
The blackbirds flute their ancient melody;
The sparrow twitters, making his small jests
High underneath the elm.

The nightingale sings happy in the leaves,
Pouring out on the winds far carrying
Her solemn melody: the sudden hawk
Quavers in the high air.

The eagle takes his flight against the sun;
High overhead the lark trills in the sky,
Down dropping from her height and changing note,
She touches earth.

Swift darting swallows utter their low cry;
The jackdaw jargons, and clear cries the quail;
And so in every spot some bird is singing
A summer song.

Yet none among the birds is like the bee,
Who is the very type of chastity,
Save she who bore the burden that was Christ
In her inviolate womb.

Mediaeval Latin Lyrics

21 THE BRIGHT AND MORNING STAR
(*Rev. 22.16*)

U p in the deep blue fields of air the great stars wheeled and burned. Jupiter and Saturn stood together in the House of the Fish for the first time in eight hundred years, and the glory of them lightened all that part of heaven. Twice eight hundred years after Christ was born, a man stood by his telescope in Prague, brooding over the lines and circles on the sheets before him. Night after night he watched, while Mars, the star of the war-god, burned his slow way through heaven to join his great brethren. And some time on a winter night in 1603 the three stars came together, and the patient watcher saw a thing that made his heart burn. For even as Mars came nearer, a new strange star, shining and changing like a precious stone, flamed for a while between Jupiter and Saturn, and slowly went out. To this man, watching, it was as though he clasped hands across a great gulf of years with those men, wise like himself in the counsels of the stars, who had stood on the flat roof of a house in an Eastern town and watched the planets wheel and the strange star burn, and knew it for the coming of a King. Once in every eight hundred years Jupiter and Saturn come together in the House of the Fish, with Mars to follow them. That they had so come, Kepler knew, but that the strange new passing star had flamed to their eyes, even as now, he could not surely know. But he wrote of what he had seen, the wonder and the mystery of it, in a book called *De Stella Nova*; and yet another wise man laid his gift at the cradle of the King.

Stories from Holy Writ

22 HOW HIGH THEY ARE!
(*Job 22.12*)

BOETHIUS

O Maker of the starry world
Who, resting on thy everlasting throne,
Turnst heaven like a spindle
And hast the stars brought under law,
So that the moon, now shining at the full,
Straight in the pathway of her brother's
flame,
Blots out the lesser stars:
Now with her crescent dim
Draws near the sun and loses all her light:
And Hesperus, in the first hour of eve,
Awakens the cold welling of the stars,
And then as Lucifer
Grows pallid in the rising of the sun.
It is thy power tempers the changing year
So that the leaves the North Wind swept away
The West Wind brings again.
Arcturus watched the sowing of the seed
That Sirius parches in the standing grain.
Naught is there that escapes the ancient law,
Or leaves the work of its appointed ward.
Thou guidest all things to their certain goal,
All but the ways of men:
Keep them in check Thou wilt not.

More Latin Lyrics

23 BY HIS SPIRIT HE HATH GARNISHED THE HEAVENS
(*Job 26.13*)

Now that the stars of the three gods, Jupiter, Saturn and Mars, stood together, about the time Our Lord was born, the records of the stars can show. But of the strange star there is no record, except that on the tables of the Chinese – for they, too, are in the counsels of the stars – there is mention of some such vanishing radiance as this, and at such a time; a record that is almost 2,000 years old.

There is no surety. Nor do we know the names of the Wise Men, though the Middle Ages made a rich legend of them. We do not know if they were kings or princes, nor whence they came. They come out of darkness into starlight, and go from starlight again into darkness. But in the starlight they are noble figures, the first of the great caravan of those who go in pilgrimage to find the King. The Chaldeans were star-gazers always; and it may be that they came from that same plain where the first Hebrew, the Man from Beyond the River, saw the sun set and the stars come out, and craved for a God who would not change and pass, and went out, not knowing whither he went, to find him. 'Abraham rejoiced to see My Day,' said Christ in the Temple; 'he saw it and was glad.' These three saw only the morning star of it; 'and when they saw the star,' says St Matthew, 'they rejoiced with exceeding great joy.'

> See how from far upon the eastern road
> The star-led wizards haste with odours sweet.

Always on the road they are, with a great dark land behind them, and the night above it brooding and mournful; but these have their faces to a star, and they are greater than men in the darkness, for they stand for the Wisdom of the world. And again in the lantern-light, kneeling, their heads bowed to the earthen floor, and their hands outstretched with their offerings to the King. There are shadows about the crib, and on their bowed heads, but the lantern light gleams on the precious things they hold. For they are the gifts that the world has always brought to its King; gold, for the glory and honour of the nations; incense, for worship; myrrh, for death.

Stories from Holy Writ

40

24 LIGHT IS SPRUNG UP
(*Matt. 4.16*)

To the Augustans, as to Dr Johnson, the gods were 'images of which time has tarnished the splendour'. But to the twelfth and thirteenth century, they have been dead and are alive again: they are part of the resurrection miracle of the Northern Spring.

For this is the amazing discovery of mediaeval lyric. Spring comes slowly up that way, but when it comes it is an ecstasy. In the North far more than in the South, Persephone comes actually from the dead. It is a new thing, and their own. With the exception of the *Pervigilium Veneris*, the spring song hardly exists in Latin literature. Here it wells up in the theological centuries very much as the lyric *Ab aestatis foribus* springs from the dry ground of the Benedictbeuern play of the Nativity. There has been a long and scholarly discussion between the Archisynagogus and St Augustine on the possibility of the Virgin Birth: a Flight into Egypt, Joseph with a prolix beard, say the stage directions, leading the Mother and Child. They are met by the King of Egypt and his *comitatus*, singing, and this is the song.

> At the gates of summer,
> Love standeth us to greet.
> The earth, to do him honour,
> Burgeons beneath his feet.
>
> The flowers that aye attend him
> Laugh at the golden prime;
> Should Venus not befriend them,
> They die before their time.
>
> Of all things the beginning
> Was on an April morn;
> In Spring the earth remembereth
> The day that she was born.
>
> And so the feast of Venus,
> Wherever Love holds sway,
> By mortal and immortal
> Is kept a holiday.

The scholars were strong in faith when they challenged Mary Virgin with that enchantment.

The Wandering Scholars

25 THE WORD WAS GOD
(*John 1.1*)

For life with all it yields of joy and woe,
Is just our chance o' the prize of learning love,
How love might be, hath been indeed, and is;
And that we hold henceforth to the uttermost,
Such prize despite the envy of the world.
The love that tops the night, the Christ in God.

The Gospel of St John has all the signs of being written last. The earlier simpler gospels are records of a thing so present and so moving that the actual telling was enough. But John had lived to see the beginnings of sophistication in the Church: to hear the Deity of our Lord questioned and denied. And so he set himself to write with one set purpose 'that ye may believe that Jesus is the Son of God, and that believing ye *may have life* through his name'. John the mystic, even in a single sentence. We only chose the facts that bore on the one great Fact: and even in the telling he stops to meditate. The last verses of Chapter 3 for instance are not the Baptist's; they are St John's commentary, and so to the end.

St John's Gospel is *Greek*. For the greater part of his life he was living in Greek-speaking Ephesus. And this thought of the *Logos* is partly Greek, partly Jewish. It's the *word* of a man as his 'expression'; just as Christ in the flesh was the Invisible made visible, so is he God become audible. Note too the peculiarly Greek conception of the *word* as *creative*. We know it is – from the artistic standpoint, even at lowest from the political. Think of a phrase like Lloyd George's 'a national Lent'. And the prophets' 'The Word was in me like a fire'. It's the urgency of *Expression*: and John is daring enough to apply it to God.

Christ to John is the vital principle of the real, psychic life of men. 'As many as received him, to them gave *he power to become* the sons of God,'[1.12].

It's the denial of cheap evangelical religion.
They receive – that they may become.
'Now are we the sons of God' – but it is a potential energy.

> Let no man think that sudden in a minute
> All is accomplished and the work is done.
> Though with thine earliest dawn thou shouldest begin it,
> Scarce were it ended in thy setting sun.

'Not as though I had already attained, and were already perfect: I press toward the mark of the prize of *the high calling of God.*'

To her brother George

26 THIS IS THE SON OF GOD
(*John 1.34*)

'Whose shoe's latchet I am not worthy to unloose.' It was a saying among the Jews that there was no service too menial for a disciple to give his Rabbi, but this fastening of the sandals. That, the disciple might not do. It shows John's sense of the transcendent relationship between him and our Lord.

When this account of John's preaching begins, he had already baptised Christ: from his saying 'I knew him not,' it seems as if he had not known his destiny, until he saw the vision.

'Behold the Lamb of God, which taketh away the sin of the world.' St John's Gospel is fuller of the great phrases of religion than any – phrases in the musical sense.

Not 'the sins', as the Litany, following an imperfect translation makes him say, but 'the sin' – the whole mass of human transgression.

'Theories manifold have been invented in order to make it plain. None of them have gone to the bottom of the bottomless.'

After all, Christ's Passion, if we believe it at all, was simply the Passion of God. 'The Atonement is a fact of eternity as well as of time' and Calvary was the eternal suffering of God made manifest for a few hours in mortal flesh – the suffering that the sin of the world always has inflicted, and will inflict to the end. And to realise it ever so little, remember the people who are taking the war hardest – poor J.D. heartsick over Roumania, make that knowledge and that sympathy infinite – and you begin to understand Gethsemane.

But that suffering has no redemptive effect unless we choose. It's like letting the men die for us in the war, and never taking it to heart. You hear people say – 'But what if at the end of it all, the world is no better than it was before it?' I suppose it's up to us. Their suffering is 'vicarious': but it rests with the people they die for whether or not it shall be 'redemptive'.

Remember that anything in Christ's life has infinity at either end of it. He is the 'Lamb slain before the foundation of the world'; the eternal travail of God: God omnipotent, but limited by his own creation, because He has made creatures so like Himself that to coerce them would be to take his divine gift from them – the free spirit of man.

To her brother George

27 TAKE MY YOKE UPON YOU
(*Matt. 11.29*)

Matthew sat down again on the doorstep. It was true. He had heard it many a time. Once a publican, always a publican. Money you had, and plenty. Yet the Man who had preached in the harbour – only yesterday they had brought a man to him lying paralysed on the broad of his back, and He said to him that his sins were forgiven him, before ever the sick man had said a word. Matthew sighed. Maybe if he were sick himself, it would give him a chance. But it wasn't likely He'd have anything to say to the likes of him. He had spoken to Peter and Andrew, and taken them from the fishing; James and John, too; and them in the very boat with their father. The old man was in a great way about it, and the season just begun. That was another reason why Matthew couldn't go near Him. Peter would have put in against him; Peter knew too much about him. The Man wouldn't have anything to say to a cheat like him. Anyhow, he was too old. There'd be nothing for it but the custom-house, and the crowd, and the smell of the harbour, all his days.

There was a sudden commotion on the road. The crowd from the preaching came streaming past, men from the harbour, women with children in their arms, all hurrying to be home for supper. Matthew got up and sat in the shadow at the back of the booth. This was what he waited for every day, the moment when the Man passed by. He sat peering out of the shadow, grey and wizened, not unlike the spider that the lame man had called him; but his eyes were eager. Gradually the crowd slackened; three or four men came together. Peter and James and John, men who were always with Him; but He was not among them. He wasn't coming. There were nights that He didn't come back to the town at all, but went off to the hills by Himself, and stayed out all night.

Matthew went to the door and looked up and down the road. It was empty again and quiet. He wasn't coming. Matthew went back and sat down again, and began to make up his accounts for the day. Suddenly a shadow fell across the light, and darkened the door. Matthew raised his head, and looked into the face of Christ.

He stood a while in the doorway, looking at him. 'Come, Matthew,' He said, and, turning, stepped into the dusty road. And Matthew rose and followed Him.

This was how Matthew found what it was to repent. And this was why, after making a great feast for the Man in his own house, and asking all his disreputable rich friends to meet Him, he left his house and his gains, to tramp the roads of Palestine. One thing only he kept – his tablets and his good clerk's hand; and sometimes at night he wrote down what the others called 'The Words'. And so, long after the Man that he followed was crucified, his notes were pieced together and made into a book; and the 'words' of Matthew the publican became the Gospel of Matthew the Saint.

Stories from Holy Writ

28 HE HAD GREAT POSSESSIONS
(*Matt. 19.22*)

The spring rains were over in the Jordan valley: in another fortnight the barley harvest would begin. It rippled, acres of it, from the terrace where their owner stood, down to the valley road, already white with dust in a world of ripening grain.

45

Once when he was reading the Roll in the synagogue – he was ruler of the synagogue, because they set his great position over against his youth – he had come on something in the Psalms that he knew: 'As the hart panteth after water brooks, so panteth my soul after Thee.' Whoever wrote that had felt what he felt. Only for himself, it was not God that he wanted. God, he dimly felt, was somewhere behind the Law. He read in the Law every day; he knew by heart Psalm 119, praising it; he supposed he ought to feel like that, about it. And when he thought of God, he thought of parchment, and a scroll of rules, about the Sabbath, and one's duty to one's neighbour. The man who wrote that Psalm wanted God; for himself, he wanted life. He had had thirty years of it, wealth and honour and marriage and friends, and he was thirsty still.

Just of late there had come a strange word to his ears – 'eternal life': a fragment of the preaching of the new prophet from Galilee. Eternal was the word you used for God; it was bigger even than everlasting, for you sometimes spoke of the everlasting hills. It sounded great enough even to satisfy him. The servants had told him last night that the prophet was staying in the village. That very day he would go to Him and ask Him what it meant.

He stood at the end of the terrace, idly watching the road winding far below him. Round the shoulder of the hill came a solitary figure, walking alone. A moment after, came a straggling company of men, walking in twos and threes. It was strange to see so many on the road; it was too early in the month for the Passover crowds. Something about the solitary figure in front held him. It must be the Prophet. He was on the road to the ford; then He must be for Jerusalem. And He might never come this way again. The young ruler made up his mind with a rush. There was a footpath through the fields that struck the road just above the ford. If he hurried he would be just in time.

So it was that in a little while the straggling following of men saw a young man running at full speed, and stood to watch his coming. His pace slackened as he neared the foremost figure. Another moment, and he was on his knees in the dusty road. The disciples came a little nearer, sympathetic and curious. His wife at the point of death, perhaps; perhaps a baby son. For himself he could want nothing; he was in too good health for that.

'Good Master,' the words came clearly, 'what good thing shall I do that I may have eternal life?'

The Rabbi stood, looking down at him.

'Why callest thou Me good?' he asked. The Rabbi did not like

46

politeness when it meant nothing. 'If thou wilt enter into life' – the young man's face brightened; this was what he wanted, life that one could enter into, like the river – 'keep the commandments.'

The young ruler's face fell. Back to the parchment and the scroll of rules. Was the way of life through the Ten Commandments? 'Which?' he asked, a little dulled.

'Thou shalt do no murder, Thou shalt not commit adultery. Thou shalt not steal, Thou shalt not bear false witness.' The young man's head went proudly up. 'Honour thy father and they mother.' Had they not died blessing him? 'Thou shalt love thy neighbour as thyself.' Surely he did. Never, to his knowledge, had he done an unkindness.

He looked at the Rabbi, doubtfully, wistfully. He had done all this, and it had made no difference.

'Master,' he said, and his voice was a little aggrieved, 'all these have I kept from my youth up. What lack I yet?'

There was a long silence. The Rabbi stood, looking down into the young man's face. Still the Rabbi gazed. So honourable a face it was, and so eager. So wide, in its desire, so narrow in the life it knew. It rolled like a map, that life, before the eyes of the shabby young Rabbi on the road, so easy a life, so prosperous, so comfortable and kindly, with a wall growing higher each year round the solitary soul. If only he would come out and leave it all behind him; use that great wealth of his not any more for his pleasure, but to save other men from pain. Not to give up, but to give away. And so to find the everlasting habitations, the love of men's hearts, the love of God.

'One thing thou lackest. If thou wilt be perfect, go and sell that thou hast and give to the poor, and thou shalt have treasure in heaven.' The voice lost its note of sternness: it no longer said 'Go.' 'And come, and follow Me.'

The head before Him was bowed. Apart from the eyes where he might have read the promise of the life that was to be, the ruler's eyes fastened on the dust of the road. Eternal life – was this eternal life, to empty one's self, to spend one's self for naught? He wanted something to make life rich. This man asked him to make it poor. Slowly he rose, his eyes fixed on the ground, and slowly he turned away.

Brightness had fallen from the air. What ailed him he did not know, though one, years after, could have told him. Like Paul, he had seen the Lord Christ, and it was hard for him to kick against the pricks. He had seen the Lord Christ; and though he was not to count all things but loss that he might win Him, he was to find that all things were a loss without Him.

The Rabbi stood a long time, looking after him. 'With men, this is impossible, but with God all things are possible.' He said it, and again took the road.

Stories from Holy Writ

29 RECONCILED TO GOD
(*Rom. 5.10*)

M en's sins were forgiven them, long before the Passion: Mary Magdalene, for instance, and the paralytic, to whom Our Lord said, 'Son, thy sins be forgiven thee.' What necessity, what reason, what need was there for the Son of God to endure such intolerable anguish, when the divine compassion was able to deliver a man from the evil one, by the sole vision of Himself? When it seems to us both cruel and unjust to demand the blood of the innocent in any kind of bargain, or to find any kind of pleasure that the innocent should be slain, how should God find the death of His Son so agreeable, that thereby He should be reconciled to the world? These, and other thoughts like them, seem to me to raise no small question as to our redemption by the death of Our Lord.

Gilles groaned aloud. 'First the Trinity,' he muttered to himself, 'and now the Atonement. That man was born to trouble, as the sparks fly upward.' He laid down Abelard's close-written sheet on his knee, and his eye travelled to the window. The sun was still low in th east: why, wondered Gilles, should this level light transfigure the earth, beyond any magic of sunrise or sunset? He saw the bare trees of the Terrain beyond the eastern wall of the cloister, the swift grey current of the Seine, and across the narrow strait the Île Notre Dame with its black piles of wood and turf, the grass between them a strange passionate green. There is more colour, he thought, in November than there is in August, except perhaps in water. The river knows it may be frozen in a week, and it runs ice-grey already. For water dies: the earth never. Those naked trees, indifferent to the fall of the leaf: the life is more than meat, they say, and the body than raiment: what we have we hold. Perhaps, thought Gilles, it was because he himself was in his November, and the last day of it too, he added with a crooked smile, that the autumn seemed to him richer than any spring, and this pale persistent sunlight had a kind of heroic tenderness. There is no memory in spring, he thought, not even the memory of other springs: but a November day of faint sunlight and emerald moss remembers all things, the wild promise of the January days, snowbroth in February, violets in March, new-mown hay in June, dew-wet mint trodden underfoot on August nights, the harvest moon in September, the hunter's moon in October. Prudentius, he thought, was the November of the poets: Prudentius remembering

> How many times the rose
> Returned after the snows.

No other poet in the world had that still clarity. It had baffled him always; he could find no metaphor that did not do violence to it, that quality neither of dawn nor noonday nor sunset. He had it now: it was this level light, of the sun near the horizon.

Sixty, when he began to write poetry, and entered the Kingdom of God. Ausonius, too, wrote his best poetry at seventy, after Paulinus broke his heart. It seems, thought Gilles ruefully, to be the condition of eternal life, for saints or for poets.

Gilles paused a moment to think that life is sadder than any graveyard: that a man is his own burial-place. Queer, queer, to see what can befall a man when he is old. Shipwreck in youth is sorrowful enough, but one looks for storms at the spring equinox. Yet it is the September equinox that drowns. A comfortable doctrine, the perseverance of the saints: a pity that so few of the comfortable doctrines were true.

So at any rate Abelard seemed to think: the comfortable doctrine of the ransom, for instance, and the debt paid once for all. Gilles returned to the neglected sheet upon his knee.

> What then is our redemption? We are justified in the blood of Christ and reconciled to God, because by the life and death of His Son He has so bound us to Himself that love so kindled will shrink from nothing for His sake. Our redemption is that supreme devotion kindled in us by the Passion of Christ: this it is that frees us from the slavery of sin and gives us the liberty of the sons of God, so that we do His will from love and not from fear. This is that fire which Our Lord said He had come to kindle upon earth.

He has never written like this, thought Gilles; his words are like burning coals.

It is the goodness of God that leads us to repentance: we grieve to have sinned against God, from love, and not from fear, less because He is just than because He is merciful. We are reconciled to God in that grief: in whatsoever hour the sinner shall grieve, says Ezekiel, he shall be saved: that is, he is made fit to be saved.

Peter Abelard

30 A SAMARITAN, AS HE JOURNEYED
(*Luke 10.33*)

ASCRIBED TO PHILIPPE DE GRÈVE

O truth of Christ,
O most dear rarity,
O most rare Charity,
Where dwell'st thou now?
In the valley of Vision?
On Pharaoh's throne?
On high with Nero?
With Timon alone?
In the bulrush ark
Where Moses wept?
Or in Rome's high places
With lightning swept?

. . . Then Love replied,
'Man, wherefore didst thou doubt?
Not where thou wast wont to find
My dwelling in the southern wind;
Not in court and not in cloister,
Not in casque nor yet in cowl,
Not in battle nor in Bull,
But on the road from Jericho
I come with a wounded man.'

Mediaeval Latin Lyrics

31 THIS DO IN REMEMBRANCE OF ME
(*Luke 22.19*)

'Ie knoweth our frame,' says the Psalmist. 'He remembereth that we are dust.' And so, in His mercy in one of those thoughts that are not as our thoughts, Christ commendeth Himself to us in the Sacrament – lest we forget.

There in the upper room, with His feet in the very shadow of the Cross that He had come so far to seek, knowing that the hands that broke the bread and poured out the wine, in gestures that had become to His disciples so familiar, would by this time tomorrow be dead hands with a wound in either palm, folded beneath linen cloths in a new tomb. Knowing all this that should befall him, our Lord looked even further into the future: looked to days when these men who had companied with him for three years would have grown old in His service, would have worn their lives out trying to set forth Jesus Christ and Him crucified to people who had never seen His face. And so looking forward, He gave them this sacrament of remembrance, to be to them an outward and visible sign that they had seen the Bread of God: that which was from the beginning, which they had heard, which they had seen with their eyes, which they had looked upon and their hands had handled – The Word of Life.

For Christ knew that it is easy for the love of many to wax cold; easy, heartbreakingly easy, to forget. There, with the agony of Gethsemane before Him and the anguish of Calvary, He knew that it would be possible, even for those who would witness it, to forget. And so without upbraiding or entreaty, He gave them this for remembrance.

We know, in our own hearts, and in relationships far less mystical, how easily *we* forget.

There are places of which we have said, 'If I forget thee, O Jerusalem!' – but life has brought us to new cities, pleasant havens, and the memory has dimmed: and it is only perhaps the blowing of some old wind, a sudden breath of new-mown hay or the smell of the burning whins, that wakens the old crying in our hearts.

Aye, and there are people we thought we could never forget: lives that we have seen go down into death, and that seemed to take half our lives

51

with them. But the graves fill up with the dust of the years, until some day you come on his name in a boy's hand in some old school book, or you find a shell that you and he quarrelled over when you were children together by the sea, and the memory of him comes in like a flood, and you cry again – 'I am distressed for thee, my brother Jonathan.' It is the little things that bring our hearts back, the little outward things that they touched and handled.

Christ drew near and walked with two disciples all the way to Emmaus, reasoning with them, reminding them of things that He had said, and their eyes were holden that they knew Him not.

> And they drew nigh unto the village and He made as though He would have gone further. But they constrained Him, and He went in. And it came to pass, as He sat at meat with them, He took bread and blessed it and brake and gave to them, and their eyes were opened and they knew Him .... They whom wisdom and truth and His spiritual Presence cannot teach to recognise Him, may be brought to recognise Him by the movement of His hands with the barley loaf, or some intonation of His voice in blessing it .... There is nothing so small but there may be attached to it some filament that will bring floating after it the whole majesty and grace of Christ and His love.

Brethren, is not this to discern the Lord's body? Sacrament after sacrament He seeks to bring us back, to remind us of a place that we had forgotten – aye, and a person too. The place is the place called Calvary and the Person – 'thou hast both seen Him, and He it is that talketh with thee'. Sacrament after sacrament, in the symbols of His body broken for us and His blood shed. He appears to us – careless, indifferent, faithless as we are – and says to us, 'Behold My hands and My feet, that it is I myself.'

'The cup of blessing which we bless, is it not the communion of the body of Christ?'

The hands that have ministered the bread and wine all down the ages since that night have been the hands of sinful men: there is no efficacy in the symbol, no grace in the ministering hands.

But remember – for this is the mystery of the Sacrament – that even as the cup is held to your lips, Diviner hands are holding a Diviner draught to your heart. The hands that minister the sacrament to your spirit are the same hands that poured out the wine in the Upper Room. And let him that is athirst, come.

Weary of earth, and laden with my sin,
I look at heaven and long to enter in.
But there no evil thing may find a home,
And yet I hear a voice that bids me come.

So vile I am, how dare I hope to stand
In the pure glory of that holy land?
Before the brightness of that throne appear?
Yet there are hands stretched out to draw me near.

It is those outstretched hands that have drawn us to His Table today.

Written jointly with her brother George for his Communion
Address after Ordination at Donaghmore, 13 June 1915.
He was to die suddenly two days later (see page 180).

32 TRUE BREAD FROM HEAVEN
(*John 6.32*)

POSSIBLY THOMAS AQUINAS

With my heart I worship,
O hidden Deity.
Thou that dost hide Thyself
Beneath these images
In full reality.

My heart submits to Thee,
Yea, all my thought:
For contemplating Thee,
All else is naught.

I cannot touch, I cannot taste, I cannot see.
All sense is cheated of Thee, but the ear.
The Son of God hath spoken: I believe:
For naught hath truth beyond the word I hear.

Upon the cross Thy Deity was hid,
And here is hidden Thy humanity:
Yet here I do acknowledge both and cry,
As the thief cried to Thee on Calvary.

I do not gaze, like Thomas, on Thy wounds,
But I confess Thee God.
Give me a stronger faith, a surer hope,
More love to Thee, my Lord.

O thou memorial of the dying Lord,
O living Bread that givest life to men,
Make strong my soul that it may live by Thee,
And for all sweetness turn to Thee again.

O Christ that gave Thy heart to feed Thy young,
Cleanse Thou my foulness in Thy blood was spilt.
One single drop of it would save a world,
A whole world from its guilt.

The veil is on Thy face: I cannot see.
I cry to Thee for grace,
That that may come to pass for which I thirst,
That I may see Thee with Thy face unveiled,
And in that vision rest.

More Latin Lyrics

33 THE LORD IS MY LIGHT
(*Ps. 27.1*)

Remember that Christ faced life and death with only the strength of a man. His way through it was as dark as to us, only for the illumination of his great faith. In the agony, He cannot see – 'If it be possible': the issue of life and death is in the hands of His God. But even in that agony, 'Abba, Father'. The word so struck the translators that they have left it in the original. His belief in his Sonship never seems to have wavered, but He was walking in a great mystery. The temptation of the wilderness, of Peter after the great recognition, are – what? The temptations of God stripped of his omniscience.

The account of Christ's earlier work is so hurried that we do not realize its long duration. 'In all the synagogues of Galilee', driven by the impulse within Him to 'other cities also, for therefore am I sent'. Yet after every access of popularity, a night alone in the open air: 'He withdrew himself into a desert place, and there prayed.'

Did Christ preach the kingdom, or did He preach Himself?

Personal notebook. Easter Saturday

My darling,

It's very early, and nobody awake: it's been raining and the light is in the drops on the plane tree, and the birds are talking. There's a faint light in the sky, as if the world wasn't yet sure that the grave would even open, and yet in its blind heart knew that it would. My darling, something I read the other day about Christ begging the others in the Garden to sit up with Him, and to pray lest they enter into temptation – 'The spirit indeed is willing' – and that He knew He was himself in extreme temptation, made the whole agony different. You know how I have harped on one's reluctance to suffer. I believe that cry, 'Let this cup pass from me', was the last knife-edge pinnacle of human dread of anguish – mental anguish too, for it was mental anguish at Calvary, even more than physical. I think we harp far too much on Christ's Godhead, make things too easy for Him that way. I believe in the Incarnation, but I believe it was a real incarnation – that the temptations to shortcuts in the wilderness were real temptations, that He was in a sense walking in the world with bandaged eyes, like the rest of us, and that He had to spend those long nights praying, to feel for the hand of God to guide Him.

To Meg (undated)

34 HE BEARING HIS CROSS WENT FORTH
(*John 19.17*)

THE WORD OF THE CROSS   PAULINUS OF NOLA

Look on thy God, Christ hidden in our flesh
A bitter word, the cross, and bitter sight:
Hard rind without, to hold the heart of heaven.
Yet sweet it is; for God upon that tree
Did offer up His life: upon that rood

55

My Life hung, that my life might stand in God.
Christ, what am I to give Thee for my life?
Unless take from Thy hands the cup they hold,
To cleanse me with the precious draught of death.
What shall I do? My body to be burned?
Make myself vile? The debt's not paid out yet.
Whate'er I do, it is but I and Thou,
And still do I come short, still must Thou pay
My debts, O Christ; for debts Thyself hadst none.
What love may balance Thine? My Lord was found
In fashion like a slave, that so His slave
Might find himself in fashion like his Lord.
Think you the bargain's hard, to have exchanged
The transient for the eternal, to have sold
Earth to buy Heaven? More dearly God bought me.

GOOD FRIDAY — PETER ABELARD

Alone to sacrifice Thou goest, Lord,
Giving Thyself to death whom Thou has slain.
For us Thy wretched folk is any word,
Who know that for our sins this is Thy pain?

For they are ours, O Lord, our deeds, our deeds,
Why must Thou suffer torture for our sin?
Let our hearts suffer for Thy passion, Lord,
That sheer compassion may Thy mercy win.

This is that night of tears, the three days' space,
Sorrow abiding of the eventide,
Until the day break with the risen Christ,
And hearts that sorrowed shall be satisfied.

So may our hearts have pity on Thee, Lord,
That they may sharers of Thy glory be:
Heavy with weeping may the three days pass,
To win the laughter of Thine Easter Day.

Mediaeval Latin Lyrics

35 THE EARTH DID QUAKE, AND THE ROCKS RENT
(*Matt. 27.51*)

ANON. ninth–tenth century

When the Lord climbed
    The gallows of the Cross,
The stars put out their light,
And darkness filled the world.

The Jews upon a reed
Gave drink to him athirst,
Vinegar mixed with mystic gall
They held before the Lord.

He breathed his spirit forth.
Death conquered all men's death,
They laid him in the grave.

The greatest Son of Man
Went seeking for the first.
He broke the gates of brass
And every bar of iron.
He walked into the dark.

A light shone in the dark,
And Adam in his bonds
Looked on the noonday sun,
And so did all his folk.

And Adam wept and cried:
'Come to our help, O Lord,
And snatch us from out these bonds.
Death keeps us in the dark.'

Strait at the Lord's command
The bonds are loosed,
And as they fall the chains
Splinter, even as ice.

At the clang of the chains
All hell quaked for dread.
It had seen its Lord
And his judgement feared.

The Lord set free
Adam and his folk,
Led them back from Hell,
Gave Paradise again.

He went back to his grave,
He rolled away the stone,
And waking in his body
The whole Christ rose again.

The Lord Christ climbed on high
Above the stars,
And sat on the right hand of his Father
With whom he reigns for ever.

More Latin Lyrics

36 A GARDEN INCLOSED
(*Song of Sol. 4.12*)

Mr Barker came on Wednesday – very big and very grave – except at intervals. And I like him as much as ever, and admire him more. Meg, we leaders had three days with him for an hour's circle, and I don't think to the end of my days that I'll forget the last one. He was urging us to look at the sheer literary beauty of the Bible – the golden phrase, and the imaginative touches. He began on Christ's life, and took this – I know you will appreciate it – where Jesus was lost and found in the Temple. And how cross and anxious and upset his father and mother were: and yet, Luke adds this: 'And Mary kept all these things in her heart.' There was silence for a while: there were just these girls of us, and himself; and then he began again. 'And the last chapters of John, but especially this, which is to me the most wonderful verse in the whole Bible: 'In the place where he was crucified there was a garden.' I don't

58

care who wrote the fourth Gospel – if the man had the insight to link together the early dawn with the last sunset, tenderness enough to see the garden where man fell, and remember it in 'the place of a skull'... 'In the place where he was crucified there was a garden.'

He stopped there, and sat quiet awhile. I don't think he could have spoken. I know we couldn't. And then he prayed.

To Meg (undated)

37 NOW IN THE PLACE WHERE HE WAS CRUCIFIED THERE WAS A GARDEN
(*John 19.41*)

I did not see it then: that awful darkness
Was on us like His shroud:
I only heard the weeping of His mother
The surging of the crowd.

Saw only, on the hill, a darker Shadow,
Outlined against the sky.
'Place of a skull' they called it, and I heard them,
Heard them, and watched Him die.

And when the night came, and it all was over,
They gave us down our Dead.
Joseph had begged it: and he brought fair linen
To wrap about His head.

And told us of a sepulchre new-finished,
Hewn in the rock near by,
It was his own; and thither then we bore Him,
The Sabbath drawing nigh.

Yet even then I thought not of the garden,
Black was the night and stark.
So Joseph held the lantern and we followed,
Bearing Him through the dark.

And suddenly the light flashed upon tree-trunks,
Leaves that were silver-gray.
So had their torches flashed upon the olives.
God – was it yesterday?

Last night, beneath the glimmer of the olives,
They took Him, and we fled.
Tonight, beneath the glimmer of the olives,
We bore our Master, dead.

★　　★　　★

Yet even then I saw not, till the breaking
Of that eternal dawn,
When I came back and found the sunlight steeping
The dew upon the lawn.

Empty the tomb, and round it white-robed angels
Under the sky and far,
The glitter of the sunrise on the olives,
The paling of a star.

And upon Calvary's sharp-smitten summit,
Clear shining after rain
Stood there the Cross, transfigured in that splendour
Its passion and its pain.

And so to me, alone in this my prison,
The vision comes again:
The primal garden of the world's first morning
Where God once walked with men.

The garden where the Master kept His vigil,
Where man his Lord betrayed,
The garden nigh to Calvary where He suffered,
Wherein the Lord was laid.

Stand they for ever in my spirit's vision,
Eternal gain and loss.
A garden, with the smile of God upon it,
And over it – a Cross.

> Poem written at Queen's University (unpublished)

38 HE IS RISEN
(Mark 16.6)

EASTER SUNDAY   SEDULIUS SCOTTUS (fl. 848–74)

Last night did Christ the Sun rise from the dark,
The mystic harvest of the fields of God,
And now the little wandering tribes of bees
Are brawling in the scarlet flowers abroad.
The winds are soft with birdsong; all night long
Darkling the nightingale her descant told,
And now inside church doors the happy folk
The Alleluia chant a hundredfold.
O father of thy folk, be thine by right
The Easter joy, the threshold of the light.

Mediaeval Latin Lyrics

39 REACH HITHER THY FINGER
(John 20.27)

THEODULF OF ORLEANS

When Christ came from the shadows by the stream
Of Phlegethon,
Scars were upon his feet, his hands, his side.
Not, as dulled souls might deem,
That He, who had the power
Of healing all the wounds whereof men died,
Could not have healed his own,
But that those scars had some divinity,
Carriage of mystery,
Life's source to bear the stigmata of Death.

By these same scars his men
Beheld the very body that they knew,
No transient breath,

61

No drift of bodiless air,
And held him in their hearts in fortress there.
They knew their Master risen, and unfurled
The hope of resurrection through the world.

By these same scars, in prayer for all mankind,
Before his Father's face,
He pleads our wounds within his mortal flesh,
And all the travail of his mortal days:
For ever interceding for His grace,
Remembering where forgetfulness were blind,
For ever pitiful, for ever kind,
Instant that Godhead should take thought for man,
Remembering the manhood of His Son,
His only Son, and the deep wounds he bore.

By these same scars his folk will not give o'er
   Office of worship, whilst they see,
     Passion, thy mystery:
   In whose dark wounds their weal,
In that descent to hell their climb to the stars,
     His death, their life,
   Their wreath, his crown of thorns.

More Latin Lyrics

40 I SEND THE PROMISE OF MY FATHER
(*Luke 24.49*)

STEPHEN LANGTON

O Holy Ghost,
Come down from heaven's height,
Give us Thy light.

O Father of the poor,
All gifts to men are Thine
Within us shine.

Comforter beyond man's comforting,
O stranger sweet
Our hearts await Thy feet.

In passion Thou art peace,
Rest for our labouring,
Our cooling spring.

O solace of our tears,
Upon the secrets of our sins and fears,
Pour Thy great light.

Apart from Thee,
Man has no truth unfeigned,
No good unstained.

Our hearts are dry.
O River, flow Thou through the parched ground,
Quicken those near to die.

Our hearts are hard,
O bend them to Thy will, Eternal Lord,
To go Thy way.

Thy sevenfold power
Give to Thy faithful folk
Who bear Thy yoke.

Give strength to endure,
And then to die in peace
And live for ever in Thy blessedness.

More Latin Lyrics

Part Three

TODAY
IF YE WILL HEAR
HIS VOICE

'For he is our God; and we are
the people of his pasture, and the
sheep of his hand. Today if ye will
hear his voice, harden not
your heart ... as in the day of
temptation in the wilderness.'

Ps. 95.7–8

41 LO, I AM WITH YOU ALWAY
(*Matt. 28.20*)

To some of us, Christ is even yet hardly risen from the dead. We think of his Resurrection as the outward and visible sign of his Divinity, the ultimate proof of the resurrection of the body, the final assurance of our eternal life. But it was something more than this that Paul meant when he said that he counted the world well lost that he might know Him and *the power of his resurrection*. It was not the thirty-three years in Palestine he was thinking of when he said that being justified by His death we are saved by His life. 'The third day he rose again from the dead: He ascended into heaven, and sitteth on the right hand of God the Father Almighty: from thence he shall come to judge the quick and the dead.' So runs the Apostles' Creed, and it has given a chill and a remoteness to our thought of Him. The men who had heard Him say that He would be with them all the days to the end, did not need to be told that they might not 'climb the heavenly steps to bring the Lord Christ down', for they knew not but that they might meet Him at every turn of the road. True, Stephen saw the heavens opened, and the Son of Man sitting on the right hand of God; but Paul saw Him also standing beside him in prison, and it was Himself and no strengthening angel that upheld him in the presence of Nero. And there is a gracious legend, that on the night before Peter's execution, his heart died within him, and he sought for a way of escape, and won his way beyond the city walls. And as he journeyed, there met him One in the darkness with His face set to Rome, who made as though He would pass by. But Peter knew Him to be the Lord and cried after Him – 'Quo vadis, Domine?' – and the old voice came back, 'I go to Rome, that tomorrow I may be crucified afresh.' 'Nay Lord', said Peter, 'but I go with Thee'; and the two of them went back to Rome together.

This vision will serve us best, the vision not of the 'King eternal, immortal, invisible', but of the Master and Sharer in our poor service, and the unwearied lover of our souls. 'Thine eyes shall see the King in his beauty; they shall behold the land that is very far off.' How could it be otherwise? Can we limit the grace of such a King to our own souls? Francis of Assisi, kneeling before the crucifix, saw the Crucified and, at

67

the same time, heard the weary call of many lands. William Carey saw Him and India; Morrison saw Him and China; Livingstone saw Him and Africa. It is the debtors of Calvary that must become the world's redeemers.

To the Christian Union (unpublished)

42 PRAY WITHOUT CEASING
(1 Thess. 5.17)

Do we realize that the Kingdom of God is the greatest thing in the world? We have our moments, some sudden conviction and distant perception of the splendour of the high calling of God. But the whole current of our lives is set the other way. 'Seek ye first the kingdom of God and all these things shall be added unto you,' said Christ, but we seek first all these things and then try to add the Kingdom of God to them. And after all, is it any wonder? For with every one of us was born the soul of the man with the muckrake – with this difference – that the muckraker had never looked up to the vision above his head: we have looked up, seen the vision, and then looked down again and lost our grip of reality. It is only when our own city of hope is both ploughed and salted that we will hark back to the city that hath foundations. 'Thou hast made sweet springs for all the pleasant streams,' cried Swinburne in his fierce anger at the cruelty of God, 'In the end Thou hast made them bitter with the sea.' And God's defence is in his anger: 'Because you have forsaken me, the fountain of living waters.' God also is wise.

But if we could have reached the water near at hand, would we have looked for it far afield? 'Sir, we had nothing to draw with and the well was deep.' It is perfectly true. James the practical tells us why. 'Ye have not, because ye ask not.' We could make no use of God, because we could not pray to Him. And we could not pray to Him because we did not believe in prayer. True, in prayer meetings and in church we pray very honestly the last three petitions of the Lord's Prayer – to give us what we want, to forgive us our sins, to keep us out of mischief – the first is usually the heartiest. But what about the three petitions that Christ put first?

A good many of us have a hazy, half-Catholic notion that prayer is excellent exercise for our souls, and if you keep at it hard enough, you may finally attain to something of what the old saints declared was communion with God. But the thing has nothing to do with pietistic vapouring. If it means anything, it means this – that we have placed in our hands a power that can influence God Himself. It is a tremendous challenge to our faith. The weakness of our religion so far has been, not that it demanded from us so much, but that it asked so little. We have forgotten that this is the mystery that overcometh the world – our faith.

That is what is wrong with us; not atheism – not agnosticism, but an imperfect faith in God. In the days before they magnified natural law one prayed with a very implicit faith for the coming of rain. In the days when the sun was our own special system of illumination it was easier to believe that one's concerns were of very vital importance to the God who made us. But when we realize with Stevenson the nature of 'this lukewarm billet on which we play our forces ... ourselves and the world we inhabit are so inconsiderable that the mind freezes at the thought'.

We may not have very much science, but when we have had to give up the blessed old conception of the clay in the Potter's hands for an age-long process of evolution with God receding farther and farther back into a Great First Cause the atmosphere of prayer becomes a little rarefied.

'Are not five sparrows sold for two farthings?' said One whom the laws of nature did not greatly terrify – 'yet not one of them falleth to the ground without your Father ...'

Is there one of us that believes that with his whole heart, who doesn't explain it to himself in the dark of his mind – we might not do it in the light – with some jargon about the Principle of Life? It is very hard to believe that the God – in Seeley's phrase – 'of the immense spaces of astronomy and the measureless ages of geology' – the God, in the Hebrew phrase, 'who inhabiteth eternity' is a God who cares for sparrows.

And yet, can He be the one and not the other? It is one of the cases in which that chilly attribute assigned to Him in the Scots' catechism becomes a quality so strong and tender and gracious. 'God is a Spirit, infinite' – therefore 'My God' just as sure as if He had no creature beside. 'Infinite' – that the strength of His omnipotence, the yearning of His compassion, might be in reach of every pair of empty finite hands.

There is yet another reason, besides this which is really the materialism of our thinking, that accounts for our dislike and distrust of prayer. It is not only that we disbelieve in God; we disbelieve in ourselves. 'Ye have not because ye ask not' says James in his downright fashion. 'Ye ask and have not because ye ask amiss.' It is a singularly accurate statement of the dilemma. For most of us were brought up on that stern and fine old preaching that would have you take the shoes from off your feet before you entered on the holy ground, though one had no vision of a burning bush. 'Betake thyself first to the ante-room and make thyself ready, ere thou canst hope to enter the Chamber of Audience: so shalt thou find thyself in the presence of the King Eternal.' There is a great truth in it: and a great stumbling block. It is as though God could only be approached in a certain attitude of mind; as though it were the old days when the petitions of the common folk must be translated into French before they could be laid before the king.

I verily believe that much of our dreary unsatisfactory prayer – and much of the wistful disappointment with which we leave the mystery of the sacrament is due to this: that we are trying to school ourselves into the proper frame of mind. One thing we are intensely conscious of – ourselves; and self-consciousness is not the road to the consciousness of God. Is it only the words that are properly winged that can reach the ear of the Eternal? One man knew better, and left on record his divine assurance. I have chosen the old Scots' version, for its old world cadences seem only to enhance the quietness and confidence that is its strength.

> O Lord, Thou hast me searched and known:
> Thou know'st my sitting down
> And rising up. Yea all my thoughts
> Afar to Thee are known.
>
> My footsteps and my lying down
> Thou compassest always
> Thou also most entirely art
> Acquaint with all my ways.
>
> For in my tongue before I speak
> Not any word can be,
> But altogether, lo, O Lord,
> It is well known to Thee.

To the Christian Union (unpublished)

43 WHERE IS GOD?
(*Job 35.10*)

The deepest need of our age, certainly the deepest need of our life, is a 'sense of God'. God is a Spirit and it is only when we *realize* Him that we worship Him in truth. For when that conviction comes upon us – though we can only count the times of its coming upon the fingers of one hand – when something has swept us below the surface on which we spend our lives into that world of the spirit that surrounds and penetrates this world that we see with our eyes and handle with our hands, that world of the spirit to which this is but

> great altar stairs
> That slope through darkness up to God –

then once for all the reasonableness of prayer is justified, and we stand 'as at the knees of God'.

It does not come often. For though we would admit, if we ever thought of it, that the 'realities of life' are not the only reality; that the stirring in our hearts when the bow cries across the strings is as real a thing as the catgut and the wood, none the less the text books will be mainly concerned with the tautness of the string. If God is not, as some have said, a prisoner in His universe, assuredly *we* are. 'The heavens declare the glory of God' and we can understand that in the empty silent spaces it was given to Mohammed to cry 'God is one'. But here, with pavements underfoot and the tinkle of tram bells and the rapid passage of a butcher's cart over the stones – one might find Him in the uttermost parts of the sea: we are prepared to believe that He fills Heaven and earth – but is He here? Are not the realities of Life meat and drink and paving-stones?

And then some night you go out from your last lecture in the gathering dusk with the gaslight flaring through the fog and the sticky pavement underfoot; and you meet them coming home through the dark, typists and clerks and shopboys, and whether it is that half revelation in the lamplight is surer than the day – or whether it is some strange influence for the sheer mass of life that is around you – but of a sudden

lifts the illusion and the truth lies bare . . .

71

At last has come the moment that came to the old prophets when they cried that God is not a God that is far off, but a God that is nigh. The very darkness becomes the brooding of His great outstretched hands, the trampling of feet and the pitiful eager voices, the very moaning of the electric wires but the cry from the creatures that He has made. 'O Lord, Thou art our Father, we are the clay, and Thou our Potter, and we all are the work of Thine hand.' Pray to Him? What madness is it that would keep us from Him? Is there anything we would make of our lives or would ask for another – what need we but to lift up our hearts with our hands to that strong and stern and gracious compulsion, and let Him do what seemeth to Him good.

'Lord, teach us to pray' said His disciples. And Jesus said 'Our Father'.

Would you prepare yourself for prayer? Then pray. There is but one conclusive answer to our doubt of Him and our diffidence of ourselves, this 'sense of God'. Nowhere do you find so overwhelming a conviction of Him as in the oldest of the sacred manuscripts, and nowhere so intense a yearning for a more intimate revelation. 'What is man that Thou shouldst set Thy heart upon him, that Thou shouldst visit him every morning and try him every moment?'

'How long wilt Thou not depart from me, nor let me alone?' There, if anywhere is 'the sense of God'. Yet hear him –

> O that I knew where I might find Him,
> That I might come even to His seat!
> I would know the words which He would answer me
> And understand what He would say unto me . . .
> Behold I go forward, but He is not there,
> And backward, but I cannot perceive Him.
> On the left hand where He doth work, but
> I cannot behold Him.
> He hideth Himself on the right hand, that
> I cannot see Him.

For here is the hopelessness of it –

> He is not a man as I am, that I should answer Him,
> Neither is there any daysman betwixt us that might
> lay his hand upon us both.

The answer to that cry is not in the last chapters of the Book of Job. It is the Incarnation of God in Christ.

'Tis the weakness in strength that I cry for! My
  flesh that I seek
In the Godhead. I seek and I find it — O Saul it
  shall be
A face like my face that receives thee; A man like to
  me
Thou shalt love and be loved by for ever. A Hand
  like this hand
Shall throw open the gates of new life to thee.
See the Christ stand!

To the Christian Union (unpublished)

44 GOD WITH US
(*Matt. 1.23*)

Invocation

Almighty God, thou art from everlasting to everlasting. Thine is the Kingdom. Honour, glory, majesty and power, are ever Thine. Thy ways are not our ways, nor our thoughts Thy thoughts. And yet Thou who dwellest in the high and holy place hast condescended to dwell also with him who is of a contrite and humble spirit. Look down upon us this day. Be present with us to bless and to guide, to comfort and to gladden, to uphold and to strengthen. Make us glad and joyful in our service: and all that we ask is in the name of Thy Son. . .

Prayer

Our Heavenly father, Thou hast assured us that as a father pitieth his children, so doth the Lord pity those who fear Him. We ask Thee in thy mercy and tender compassion to lend thine ear now and hear us as we come to Thee. We would remember before Thee our many blessings, and would ask Thee to accept this poor thanksgiving. We bow before Thee acknowledging that our praise can never fulfil our sense of thy divine goodness. But we praise Thee that Thou dost look behind words to the motives that underlie them, and hast brought us safely to this day. We would bless Thee that thy love is wisdom. We finite creatures ask for finite things, and Thou hast given us infinite things; we ask for the petty trivialities of a day: Thou hast given us what money cannot buy; we ask for protection and safety for the day: Thou hast given it, and hast assured us of protection and safety for eternity. We would praise Thee for thy love which Thou dost daily manifest to us, but which Thou hast fully shown in its most perfect light in thy dear Son, our Lord and our Saviour, Jesus Christ. May He dwell in our hearts and in our lives.

To the Christian Union (unpublished)

45 I WILL COME TO YOU
(*John 14.18*)

There is one more thing that the older Church has got, and that we have not – and it accounts for a good deal of our faithlessness in prayer. 'If ye had known who it was,' said Christ, 'ye would have asked.' We did not know who it was, we have lost what the early Church could realize so keenly – the belief in the abiding presence of Christ. We pray for the indwelling of the Holy Ghost. It was Himself that Christ promised us – and it was to Himself that He told us to come when we wanted Him, though He said that the Holy Spirit would tell us what to say to Him.

It was this devotion to what they quaintly called the Person of Christ that made the Society of Jesus in its foundation so great a school for missionaries and martyrs. And this, I believe, is to this day the greatest strength of the Roman faith – that week by week, Christ's lovers believe that they receive Him in the Sacrament. This is the realizing faith that we have lost. 'I do not wonder,' says Ruskin, 'at what men suffer, but I wonder often at what they lose.'

Was it hard to worship the Father in spirit and in truth?
The Word became flesh, and dwelt among us.

Was it hard to find audience of the King Eternal?
This Man receiveth sinners, and eateth with them.

Was it hard by searching to find out God?
Seeking us His worn feet hasted.

74

And so, if you would have a 'school of prayer', take the road to Emmaus. It does not very much matter that your brain is numb and your heart is dead, and all you can say of Him is that Jesus of Nazareth was a prophet mighty in word and deed. Have somewhat to say to Him, if it is only that you trusted it had been He who should have redeemed Israel: it does not matter as long as you say it to Himself. They were not likely subjects, these two, for a divine revelation; they were a pair of disheartened sceptics. But they were talking about Him: their minds were occupied with Him. 'And it came to pass' – as it always does come to pass – 'that Jesus Himself drew near and went with them'. 'And they knew Him not'. Is any story in the Gospels so gracious as this – that day after day a man may walk the roads with Christ, and know Him not. And in the end something as commonplace as this presence of a Third in a wayside inn, some sudden uplift of heart, some compunction at the memory of an unkindness spoken or done, some heartache in the day of your triumph, may serve for the breaking of bread.

They whom wisdom and truth and His spiritual Presence cannot teach to recognize, may be led to recognize Him by the movement of His hands with the barley loaf, or some intonation of His voice in blessing it. . . . There is nothing so small but there may be attached to it some filament which will bring after it the whole majesty and grace of Christ and His love.

'Watch therefore: for ye know not the day nor the hour when the Son of Man may come.'

To the Christian Union (unpublished)

46 IN SPIRIT AND IN TRUTH
(*John 4.24*)

The tiny bell on the church had begun to ring, summoning these tiny souls, hedgers and ditchers and shambling old men and women with child, to sit down with Apostles and Martyrs, St Ambrose and St Augustine and the unnumbered *manes* of the unnamed holy dead. And listening, a great longing took him [Abelard] to go in and sit among them: to feel no more the outcast, the man whom God had rejected and

75

would have no longer to serve Him seized him: he sat down on the stone ledge of the porch to take breathing space and courage to go in. The Alleluia was just ending: there was a pause, and Herluin's hoarse relaxed voice began the Gospel, reading aloud the Beatitudes that are for broken men, for men that are poor in spirit, for men that mourn, for men that hunger and thirst after righteousness, for men that are reviled and all manner of evil spoken against them falsely. *Rejoice and be exceeding glad, for great is your reward in heaven.* Well, he was broken enough, he had mourned, he had hungered and thirsted after righteousness, at any rate after truth, there had been evil enough said of him. But he was not blessed. There were some that God rejected, and He had rejected him.

Then fell a silence, then Thibault's young voice, the boys' voices following it. '*The souls of the just are in the hand of God, and the torment of malice shall not touch them: in the sight of the unwise they seemed to die, but they are in peace.*'

He rose and went quietly out of the porch and past the quiet graves. The torment of malice had touched him: the hand of God was not for him. The whole gentleness of the November day, the day that seemed to him more than any other to have Good Friday's peace, dreamt above the world, but not on him. He had no anger now, no bitterness even. He had blasphemed God once, but he blasphemed no more. '*Though He slay me, yet will I trust in Him,*' – why did they never finish that sentence as Job finished it? – '*but I will maintain my ways before Him.... My righteousness I hold fast, and I will not let it go.*'

He halted suddenly, for in this queer silence of the earth, with all the saints intent upon the prayers of the faithful, and all the world droning with devotion like a hive of bees, now if ever it seemed to him that he might speak and God would hear, with only they two left face to face. He stood quiet and grim, his face turned to the quiet sky. All the traditions of his faith, all the memories of his life were forcing him upon his knees, but he would not. His mother's silent abnegation, the humility of his father's walk with God, the whole divine consolation of psalmist and prophet pleaded with him in vain. '*As far as east is distant from the west, so far hath He removed our transgressions from us.*' Let him first be shown wherein he had transgressed. '*Like as a father pitieth his children, so the Lord pitieth them that fear Him.*' He asked for no pity, he asked for justice, the justice that a man would give his fellow, aye, that a lord would give his serf.

And standing there, braced against heaven, the wind that had blown upon him once and been forgotten, breathed upon him again. It came without observation, for the kingdom of God is within: a frail wisp of memory, voiceless as the drift of thistle-down, inevitable as sunrise. *'Neither do I condemn thee: go, and sin no more.'*

He saw no heavens opened: he saw no Son of Man. For a moment it seemed to him that all the vital forces in his body were withdrawing themselves, that the sight had left his eyes and the blood was ebbing from his heart: he felt the grey breath of dissolution, the falling asunder of body and soul. For a moment: then his spirit leapt toward heaven in naked adoration. Stripped of all human emotion, with no warmth of contrition, with no passion of devotion, but with every power of his mind, with every pulse of his body, he worshipped God.

Peter Abelard

Part Four

PREACH
THE GOSPEL TO
EVERY CREATURE

'And he said into them, Go ye
into all the world, and preach the
gospel to every creature.'
Mark 16.15

47 GO YE INTO ALL THE WORLD
(*Mark 16.15*)

I have been working all day at the baptism of Cornelius. I was almost sure that there was going to be no illumination, only an obvious all-over transparency. What first redeemed it from that rather flat light was something in the accent of Peter's question – that was yet no question, a sort of awe. 'Can any man forbid water that these should not be baptized, which have received the Holy Ghost as well as we?' It echoed something that I could not fix, and at last I found it:

> Then felt I like some watcher of the skies,
> When a new planet swims into his ken.
> Or like stout Cortez when with eagle eyes
> He star'd at the Pacific – and all his men
> Looked at each other with a wild surmise –
> Silent, upon a peak in Darien.

I think they had thought of their new faith as the Jordan, in whose waters men might be healed. And now Peter saw it when it met the sea; and for a little while the tide is broken and discoloured with the old sediment, and the rush of the river keeps its current visible a little way: but around it and beyond it – 'the multitudinous seas encarnadined',

'What was I that I should withstand God?'

I have never more respected the greatness of that early Church: instead of the supremacy which Messiah was to have brought them, an equality that they had never before given. And yet – they glorified God, because that to the Gentiles also was granted repentance unto life.

And Joppa, where Peter saw the vision and the sea, reminded me of that other missionary, the unwilling one, who left Joppa for Tarshish. I looked up George Adam Smith, and got an amazing illumination on Jewish prejudice. Do you remember, 'With magnificent reserve he has not gone further; but only told unto the prejudiced faces of his people that out there, beyond the Covenant, in the great world crying in darkness, there live, not beings created for ignorance and hostility to God, elect for destruction, but men with conscience and hearts, able to turn at His word and to hope in His mercy – that to the farthest ends of the world and even on the high places of unrighteousness, Word and mercy work, just as they do within the Covenant.'

And the last sentence of the book: 'God has vindicated His love, to the jealousy of those who thought it was theirs alone. And we are left with this grand vague vision of the immeasurable city, with its multitude of innocent children and cattle, and God's compassion brooding over all.'

To Dr Taylor, 17 February 1918

48 WHY THIS WASTE?
(Mark 14.4)

Dear,

It's Sunday evening, and all afternoon I have been reading George Adam Smith's 'Isaiah'. He has been very good for me. I am going to take it up for a while instead of Maclaren on the Gospels. It is good to be shaken up – and Isaiah does it. Of late it has been the Gospels, and only the Gospels, and it is so easy to make them 'a very lovely song of one that hath a pleasant voice'.

You were right when you said that sharing other people's sadness helped one's own. I know now the thing that pulled me out of the depression that was on me was going up to the country to see two dear old people who were very good to me when I was little. Times are harder for them now than then; they have 'set the land' and are living on in the old house alone. And thanks to you, I was able to help them a wee bit. Somehow coming up against real worry and the patient sadness of old age that has nothing to hope for here – it cured me of 'malingering'. And God bless you for those verses – I found the letter that had them just after I wrote begging for them.

> Somewhere thou livest and hast need of Him . . .
> Oh true brave heart, God keep you, whereso'er
> In God's wide universe thou art today.

Tomorrow I have my circle: 'the ordination of Barnabas and Saul'. I am working it more or less on the lines of 'To what purpose was this waste?' Peter and John, left to defend the faith in the high places of Judaism, and Paul, with his scholarship and eminence sent out to pagan cities where all that Rabbinical eloquence availed him nothing: where he must rely on nothing but the bare facts of the story, and his vision of the Person – and the power of the Holy Ghost. It was better for him of course. And after all, the erudition and the eminence stood him stead in a different quarrel, not Christ against the Rabbis, but the Gentiles against the 'circumcision'. It *did* cheer me to find that immense scholarship being used at last: and what would have befallen the faith if the Gentiles had had a weaker champion.

The 'application' is, I think, the whole question of vocation. I have two quotations: one, from I don't know where – 'The surest method of arriving at God's purpose for us is to find the right use of the present moment. Our present grace is the most infallible will of God.' The other is that faultless last paragraph of George Eliot's *Middlemarch*:

> Her finely touched spirit had still its fine issues, though they were not widely visible. Her full nature, like that river of which Cyrus broke the strength, spent itself in channels which had no great name on the earth. But the effect of her being on those around her was incalculably diffusive: for the growing good of the world is partly dependent on unhistoric acts: and that things are not so ill with you and me as they might have been, is half owing to the number who lived faithfully a hidden life, and rest in unvisited tombs.

To Dr Taylor, 19 September 1915

49 HEBREW OF THE HEBREWS
(*Phil. 3.5*)

Stephen; Stephen. The old pain surged again about Saul's heart. Would that wound never heal? Though there were worse things to remember than Stephen's face. There was the face of the man they had brought before him, after scourging, to recant. He had said after Saul the words of recantation, had cursed Jesus of Nazareth for a blasphemer and an impostor. Saul's hands twisted together. Was he never to be free? To the end of his days would that knife turn in his heart? It might have happened yesterday. 'O Lamb of God that takest away the sins of the world, have mercy upon us.' He had had mercy. It might be that this very agony was His mercy too: but there were days when it seemed more than Saul could bear.

> With them into God's house I went,
> With voice of joy and praise,
> Even with the multitude that kept
> The solemn holy days.

For a moment Saul's mind flashed back, almost wistfully, to the old untroubled days, when his way had lain so straight before him, when he had stood here and thanked God for his name and race, his self-control and his honour, when his thoughts went up with the sunlight on them in praise of a God made in Saul's own image. Well, he had seen Him since. 'Wherefore I do abhor myself, and repent in dust and ashes.'

Some things, at least, he had saved out of the shipwreck of his pride. That keen brain, the swordplay of his wit, his merciless logic, his knowledge of the Law − they would taste the edge of it yet, these men who had made a mock of his Lord. Out of their own Scriptures would he condemn them. As for Peter and James and that silent John − they were better men than he, but they were not scholars: they had not Saul's traditions. No wonder that they had made little impression on the learned men of Jerusalem. Not until Saul came back had he realised how hungry he had been for the curial speech, for the clash of dialectic: in the first crash of debate he felt himself again a swimmer in strong familiar seas. Already, he knew, he had kindled more fury in the synagogues than Peter and the rest in three years. Fury: but was not that very fury a sign of his efficacy? And the end? Martyrdom perhaps, and a fitting expiation, if Stephen's slayer might atone by it for Stephen's death. But surely, in the strategy of God, who so fit to convert Jerusalem as Saul the persecutor?

Yet still the oppression deepened upon Saul. Twilight had fallen: he was solitary and the silence of the court closed round about him, shutting him off from all the kindly life that was beyond those walls. Loneliness came upon him, a worse loneliness than he had felt since that awful solitude in Damascus, when he had lain for three days, dark at noon. Three days, until he heard the blessed feet coming through the doorway, pausing at last by his side. Even as those footsteps were coming now. So strong was the memory upon Saul that he turned, half expecting to see again the kindly venerable face that had looked down upon him and blessed him. But it was not Ananias. It was the Lord Christ. 'Make haste,' He said, 'and get thee quickly out of Jerusalem; for they will not receive thy testimony concerning Me.'

Saul was on his knees, pleading for his life. 'Lord,' he urged, 'they know that I imprisoned and beat in every synagogue them that believed on Thee, and when the blood of Thy martyr Stephen was shed, I was standing by and consenting unto his death, and kept the raiment of them that slew him —'

The words died. Christ had turned from him, was gazing through the open archway, past the grating with the notice on it, into the night outside.

'Depart,' He said, 'for I will send thee far hence unto the Gentiles.'

Silently Saul rose, and went out, under the archway, past the grating. At the top of the steps he paused. What compulsion was this that had driven him out, without leave-taking, without a word of blessing to heal his hurt? He turned to come back, but the temple was empty. Empty, as Saul's own heart. He had heard sentence of banishment, sentence of death, death to his hopes, his scholarship, his ambition. Banishment from the streets that were like the veins of his body, from the Temple that was his heart. What had he to bring to the Gentiles to whom the Sacred Books were hardly a name, and all that vast argosy of learning, the very Ark of God, no better than a derelict half sunk? Nothing but — Saul's heart stood still. Nothing but the Christ that he had that moment seen. He stood on the steps of the Temple, face to face with the blue vault of heaven with its stars, Jerusalem a huddle of lights at his feet, and the uttermost horizon seemed too narrow for the tides that swept about his heart.

'God forbid that I should glory save in the cross of Christ Jesus my Lord, through whom the world is crucified unto me and I unto the world.'

Stories from Holy Writ

50 OF WHOM SPEAKETH THE PROPHET?

(*Acts 8.34*)

'The place of the scripture which he read was this, He was led as a sheep to the slaughter; and like a lamb dumb before his shearers, so opened he not his mouth. And the eunuch answered Philip and said, I pray thee, of whom speaketh the prophet this? Of himself, or of some other man?'

It's curious how slowly a lesson illuminates; for days there is a veil upon it, but always in the last day or two it grows incandescent.

This time it is Philip, on the road to Gaza 'which is desert'. It struck me as a very dramatic story: a perfect thing to do with children in sand. As far back as I remember I saw it in my head. But because of its very picturesqueness I doubted if I'd get much out of it. And I was distressed by the title given in the International leaflet – 'The First African converts'.

But that quotation from Isaiah is like a well. And I began to see how that strange chapter must have haunted the eunuch's ears. It was no wonder that he should have been reading Isaiah, for he is the prophet of the Gentiles. I have sometimes thought that so much of the Old Testament must have seemed a little aloof from the proselytes: not Isaiah.

I have been reading George Adam Smith again. I had never noticed before how the Dawn song 'Awake, awake, put on thy strength O Zion' goes out into silence before this; and one forgets even 'Jerusalem the Holy City'. I see the thing almost like the fragment of a Greek play, with two voices answering, and a chorus of sorrowful ransomed men. Do you remember that marvellous paragraph:

> Most wonderful and mysterious of all is the spectral fashion in which the prophecy presents its Hero. He is named only in the first line and once again: elsewhere He is spoken of as He, we never hear or see himself. But all the more solemnly He is there: a shadow upon countless faces, a grievous memory on the hearts of the speakers. He so haunts all we see and all we hear that we feel it is not Art, but conscience, that speaks of Him.

And if He is not named, no more are the other figures. It is 'He' and 'us all'. At first one sees 'many nations': and then all thought of them as spectators vanishes, and it is all men's hearts that are pierced because of Him. Read it as he did – the Ethiopian: he could not wholly share in the 'brightness of thy rising'. But he could come, with all men, into the shadow of this mystery and sorrow.

To Dr Taylor, 3 February 1917

51 MERCY FROM EVERLASTING
(*Ps. 103.17*)

I have been working all afternoon at the Riot in Jerusalem. What I like best in it is Paul's craving for Pentecost in Jerusalem. I think somehow every fresh sight of the city must have been a new baptism of pain – and of the Holy Ghost. I'm using it to insist on the value of association of times and seasons and sacraments – you know that sentence of Maclaren's:

> They whom wisdom and truth and His spiritual presence cannot teach to recognize Him, may be brought to it by the movement of His hands with the barley-loaf, or some intonation of His voice in blessing it. There is nothing so small but there may be attached to it some filament that will bring floating after it the whole majesty and grace of Christ and His love.

My paper on The Forgiveness of Sins? Here is a scrap: 'We tolerate cheap thinking about religion, as we tolerate it about nothing else, and in nothing has our thinking been so cheap as in this article of the Creed. How many of us translate "the forgiveness of sins" by "the remission of the consequences"? We deserved to be punished: Christ took our punishment: and so God lets us off. This is our travesty of the most poignant verses in Holy Writ. We have bridged the abyss of the passion of God with an easy metaphor: clutched at security: and over against that ignominy, this faith that refuses shelter, that chooses to pay to the uttermost farthing, has something fine about it, yet only comparatively fine. It opposes to a cheap thought of sin a thought only less cheap.

87

'For there is another attitude beside these: a faith that will pay to the uttermost farthing, and when the debt is cancelled, feel there is something broken yet. David, his punishment ended, going down to the House of God to cry: "Cast me not utterly from thy presence"; the prodigal expiating in hunger and hardship and shame the sins of youth, and on his lips the cry, "no more worthy to be called thy son". In what coin of penalty will Peter pay, that he may face the Risen Christ true man again?

'Ah God! Ah God! That it were possible
To undo things done. To call back yesterday!

'There is nothing in all the world deep enough to call to that deep but those unfathomable sentences: "As far as east is distant from the west, so far has He removed our transgressions from us." Unfathomable, because their soundings are in that Eternity in which our yesterdays and tomorrows are one.'

To Dr Taylor, 23 September 1918

52 NEITHER ROBBERS, NOR YET BLASPHEMERS
(Acts 19.37)

I've the lesson 'Great is Diana of the Ephesians' today. Can't you think how hopeless it seemed to Gaius and Aristarchus for instance, Paul himself maybe, to hear that tumultuous pagan shout for hours, and the whole city in carnival – an Eastern carnival and an Eastern May: one's self is so hopeless sometimes, when you think of the big religions entrenched against us – even with our organized church and a Christian continent behind us. And behold 'this Paul' with nothing but the urgency of the heat in him, and his personal experience of God, out against the whole earth. And the admirable formality of the town clerk, the tact and the indulgence and the grand manner of the governing classes: so great he must have seemed, and the battered vagabond preacher so little – and now he is only remembered because for half an hour he was caught into the current of the will of God. 'The world passeth away and the lust thereof, but he that doeth the will of God abideth.'

I got my illumination for Tuesday's class just the night before. It came in a flash before I slept. It was Christ's promise of 'treasures in heaven'. Take all His teaching on money, and that follows it – even the much-vexed parable about the unjust steward. It is to use it to win love, 'the everlasting habitations', for of all things that abide, Love only has eternity. That was what the ruler lacked: it wasn't renunciation that our Lord demanded, it was consecration. The thing condenses into a phrase: Christ does not ask us to 'give up'; He asks us to *give away*'. It's the parable of The Talents again. What you have you are not to renounce, and bury: you are to *use*. And the 'treasure in heaven' – it was a new world that Christ was calling him into, 'for he that loveth, dwelleth in God, and God in him'. That story is the meeting-ground and the battle-ground of asceticism and Christianity. Before, I always saw it as the bulwark of the monastic ideal. But don't you love the other way of it?

To Dr Taylor, 29 April 1918

53 GRACE, SEASONED WITH SALT
(*Col. 4.6*)

'Let the small coin of your courtesies have the stamp of the King's Mint. Let your familiar speech have the savour of the King's garden.' The most conspicuous thing in Acts 27 is the extraordinary charm of St Paul. One thinks of him too much as rabbinical theologian, and keen debater, and strict disciplinarian. You have to admit his passionate friendships: cf. Philippians 2.27 about Epaphroditus – 'Indeed he was sick nigh unto death: but God had mercy on him; and not on him only, but on me also, lest I should have sorrow upon sorrow.' But in this chapter of Acts, it's Paul, the unofficial Paul, not with converts or churches or assemblies, but among absolute strangers: Paul in a new set. And before all is done, they're listening to the little man like a kinder sort of Buddha. It's your old priest in *Kim* with Luke as his 'chela', making absolute conquest of a young lieutenant who is bringing him to London for trial, with a gang of seditious prisoners, and a lascar crew. He got to care for them awfully. You can see that he was praying for every man of them by the answer: 'God hath *given* thee all them that sail with thee.'

Hear the nice old voice of him: 'Wherefore I pray you to take some meat, for this is for your health'. Whether he won Julius or not, it does not say. He certainly won his heart. Even in the crash at the end, he is willing to risk his military reputation by the escape of the prisoners (a Roman soldier answered for his prisoners with his life), rather than have Paul killed.

Unless you give your mind to being kind to everybody, you will often be cruel to somebody.

For the Girls' Auxiliary

54 PAUL CAME TO CORINTH
(*Acts 18.1*)

It was very quiet in the house of Justus; the only house in Corinth that was quiet that night. For it was May, and the third day of the Isthmian games was over. While they lasted, Corinth never went to bed. Paul stood by the window of the house of Justus, looking out. At the end of the street the water of the harbour lapped, black and evil, on the landing stage; the harbour that made Corinth the market of the world. It was so far off, the Palestine where the Man he preached had lived and died; the little country of hill-roads and green pastures where He had spent his days in footsore journeying, the Holy City where they crucified Him. It was easy to preach Him in Jerusalem where men knew the story, where they had loved Him or hated Him. But here, where no one cared, where His very name had to be translated, to speak of Him here among their thousand gods, wealth that the Man of Nazareth had never seen, sins of which His holiness had never dreamed – it was to preach a shadow, from a quiet world of shadows.

For a long time he stood, and the silence in the room grew. A strange quiet fell on him. Outside the torches still flared, the flutes still maddened the night, but the throbbing in his head had stopped. Paul raised his head with a long sigh, and saw the Lord Christ. He stood at the window, grey in the shadow, looking out at the street; and the torchlight

90

flickered on His quiet face as it might flicker on heaven with its stars. He looked at the street below him, but it seemed to Paul that He saw Corinth, and beyond Corinth the illimitable reaches of the world. Not bitterly, not sorrowfully, but as a man looks at that which will some day be his.

'Be not afraid, Paul,' He said at last, as though He answered the long night's distress. 'Speak, and hold not thy peace. For I am with thee.' He still stood, looking out. 'I have much people in this city,' He said, and so passed out.

A long while after, Paul rose and stood again by the window. The torches were burning low, but the flutes still quickened, and Paul heard a new thing in them, the weariness of the players, jerking their hearts out for their daily bread. All the noises of Corinth rose about his ears, the strange mournfulness of a city that is making merry. And it seemed to him that they blended into one great cry. 'O God, Thou art our Father. We are the clay, and thou our Potter, and we all are the work of Thy hand. Be not wroth very sore, O our God.' He stood, stretching out his hands, his heart breaking. Children of devils? Nay rather, children of God.

Stories from Holy Writ

55 IN THE LIKENESS OF SINFUL FLESH
(*Rom. 8.3*)

Acts 28.4: 'When the barbarians saw the venomous beast hang on his hand, they said, No doubt this man is a murderer ... but when they saw no harm come to him, they changed their minds, and said he was a god'; cf. Acts 14.11: 'The gods are come down to us in the likeness of men.'

Curiously enough, those same regions of Asia Minor about Lystra are the background of a beautiful old legend in Ovid. It's awfully like the story of the three angels coming to Abraham, and foretelling the birth of Isaac. Here Jupiter and Mercury and a third god – I forget him – walked through the fields and stopped to ask for a drink from an old man at his cottage door. And he brought them in and entertained them, and they found that he and his old wife had no son. And they gave him one – and went their way.

There was surely something at the back of that instinct – to look for a God in the likeness of men. They have it in India to this day. Ram and Krishna are gods now, but in their day they were men, not quite perfect men, and so there is a Hindu festival where the continual invocation is, 'By the faith of the Sinless Incarnation.' It is the belief of India that some day the Sinless Incarnation will come. 'What will ye, if it be come already?'

And the extraordinary thing is, that a belief in the Incarnation of God should have arisen in a people like the Jews, fiercely monotheistic: who accounted the likening of God to his creatures as hideous blasphemy. The intolerance of Islam of the claims of Christ is the *natural* attitude of the Semitic races – Mohammed is of course a Semite, just like the Jews themselves. If the belief had risen in India, one could discount it readily, for it is the natural soil for faith in a God come in the flesh; it is naturally pantheistic. But the Jews were not; especially after idolatry had been pumped out of them by the fearful discipline of the exile and the return. That *Jews* should begin to believe in a 'God manifest in the flesh' is a tremendous argument that He was so manifest; and a tremendous testimony to the efficacy of the Person of Christ.

To Dr Taylor, 6 May 1918

56 OTHER SHEEP I HAVE
(*John 10.16*)

Binzuru is not sanctified: he is only popular. When Buddha and the fifteen Rakkan sit inside the chancel, Binzuru sits outside. The fifteen Rakkan are the disciples whom Gautama chose that he might impart to them the Doctrine, and now being perfect in holiness and the extinction of desire, they are even as Buddha. They sit with him in the half-light behind the chancel grating, where the air is blue with incense smoke and vibrant with prayer intoned, and the worshippers come and go with unshod feet. But Binzuru sits in the outer court where the wooden 'geta' click all day on the pavement, and the light is broad and strident with much conversation. Once there were sixteen Rakkan, but Binzuru was the sixteenth.

It is so long ago that he has almost forgotten it himself; yet once Binzuru was indeed a saint, and one whose feet were far advanced upon the Way. Then came the day that he sat, and a fellow-disciple with him, and contemplated the Infinite. The fellow-disciple may well have been Daruma the Legless, who still sits near Binzuru, the chancel screen between; having sat for a matter of nine centuries his lower limbs dropped off, being atrophied by disuse, absorbed into the Infinite Negation.

Binzuru sat and contemplated. Always when possible the disciples sat under a fig tree to contemplate. Gautama established the precedent; also it casts a broad and quiet shadow. This day the shadow was grey and dead in a world that was white with heat. Binzuru saw through half-closed eyes the universe sweep from him in rhythmic colourless waves. A woman came through the grove and stepped into the sunlight on the road. She swayed as she went. Binzuru saw her pass. The waves still rose and fell but they were no longer colourless. Binzuru's eyes went after her. Gradually the world steadied itself; she was the only thing that swayed. Binzuru still gazed after her, not knowing what he did; then in his abstraction he spoke aloud. He said, 'She is very beautiful.'

The voice of Binzuru came to Daruma from a great way off, but it conveyed to him with an intimate shuddering that his sainted brother was overtaken by mortal sin. He went and told the Buddha. Binzuru was disgraced; Binzuru bowed himself and went out.

So then Binzuru sits outside the chancel, and sometimes of a moonlight night, though of late it has happened seldom, he sees again the swaying of the shoulders that cost him the Bodhisat.

Prose version of 'The Spoiled Buddha' (unpublished)

> She stood in her scarlet gown,
> If any one touched her
> The gown rustled.
> Eia.
> She stood, her face like a rose,
> Shining she stood
> And her mouth was a flower.
> Eia.
> She stood by the branch of a tree,
> And writ her love on a leaf.

More Latin Lyrics

93

57 PHYSICIAN, HEAL THYSELF
(*Luke 4.23*)

I am not going to begin this paper with the Man from Macedonia. The vision that the Church sees today is not the vision that was given to the greatest of all missionaries in Troas by the Aegean. The cry of the non-Christian religions is no longer an appeal, it is a defiance – Macedonia is no longer supplicant – she is at bay. 'Come over and help us' was her summons to the Church for nineteen centuries; and thanks to that Church's indifference, 'Physician, heal *thyself*' is her word for us today. It is in the vision of our older seer that we find the truer parallel. When Isaiah saw a power that had shared in the very fullness of God brought to the verge of dissolution – 'Sheol from beneath is moved to meet Thee at Thy coming; it stirreth up the dead for Thee, it hath raised from their thrones all the Kings of the nations. All they answer and say unto Thee – "Art Thou also become one of us? Art Thou weak as we?"'

It is no imaginary challenge – it is echoed and re-echoed in page after page of the journalism of the East; it is confirmed and reinforced by the non-Christian literature of the West. The whole current of the world is setting against belief in the supernatural; one by one it has undermined the old religions of the East, and one by one they have crumbled and gone under. And now the agnostics of both East and West assure us that Christianity itself is going out with the tide.

'Buddhism,' says a famous Japanese scholar and agnostic, 'in spite of its former grandeur, is now practically a Colosseum magnificent in ruin. Most educated Japanese are agnostics.' Confucianism is an empty husk – 'we have a mass of ceremonies' says a Chinese newspaper – 'but we have no religion'. The history of religions in India has been described as three thousand years of tragedy and defeat. In the waveless sea of Islam itself there is an undercurrent of dissatisfaction that is driving its men of intellect – not into Christianity – but into agnosticism. Agnosticism is the goal to which the East is heading – not Christianity. And why?

Because the East will have none of a religion that has been discredited by the West. We cast off our own faith, say the Eastern nations, because it failed to dominate *your* civilization. We had a great creed; and we out-grew it; you had a great creed – perhaps a greater, and you are out-

94

growing it. Our thinking men have broken our idols and left our temples desolate; your thinking men, your Herbert Spencer, your John Morley, your Leo Tolstoi have shaken the dust of your churches from off their feet. As a matter of fact, it was they who showed us the way.

You condemned our religions, because they did not influence our morality; we condemn your religion, because it does not influence your morality. Do you know that the seaports when your Christian sailors come are the very plague spots of our East? That the first criminals tried in the Japanese law courts were Europeans – for murder and adultery. If we had not seen we might have believed. But you forget that we, as well as you, have learned agnosticism at Oxford and Cambridge; and that we as well as you have seen London and Manchester and Birmingham. We, as well as your Ruskin, have seen 'The immeasurable, unimaginable guilt, heaped up from hell to heaven', of what you are pleased to call your great industrial centres; and the thing that impressed us most, as well as your Canadian journalist – was the 'mirthless, wordless, *hopeless* face of the common crowd; the social problem, appalling even to despair.' What does all this mean, if not that Christianity has played itself out? You said yourselves at your great Edinburgh conference, that the reason why so few of your men are volunteering to come and preach to us, is that so few of your men are coming into your church at all. You said yourselves that the greatest hindrance to your work among us was the state of your church at home – and you never said a truer word. You said yourselves that something had got to happen to your church at home if it was even going to look at the work that lay before it. Most assuredly something would need to happen. But it is not going to happen.

Of course you will make a frantic effort at reform, just as Buddhism is doing, modernizing her creed and purging her abuses; just as Hinduism is doing, with her Arja Somai and Brahma Somai, and her desperate striving after a spiritual national religion. But it is your death throe. 'The Dawn comes but once to awaken a man,' say the Africans truly, 'and you will not find a rebirth of your own faith'. The Dawn comes but once – and you as well as we, are moving into the light of common day. And after all, you will find daylight a better working medium than the emotional splendours of the sunrise; and you will soon be heart-whole in the service of the great reality, 'Substance, the alpha and omega, the lord god almighty of our naturalistic creed'. By your own confession, it is the acknowledged creed of thousands in Europe already – and the unacknowledged creed of thousands more. The case for the prosecution is closed.

Since Christianity has been given a fair trial side by side with the religions of the East, since like them she claimed to dominate life and has not done so, since like them her decay is most manifest in those countries where she most flourished, since she has been submitted to the same practical tests and has failed – it is generally accepted that there is 'no essential difference between the religions of the civilized world'. And since the founder of it claimed to be omnipotent and is impotent, since he claimed divinity and has failed humanly – that he be stripped of his divine honours. But in as much as he was a great teacher, that he be placed side by side with other great teachers, Buddha and Confucius, and the Hinde sages – or, to please the Hinde brethren – the Hinde incarnations. And that it be generally accepted that his day is past.

To the Christian Union (unpublished).

They have crucified their Lord afresh
Upon another cross.
His wounds are new again
The Tree of Life is lost...
O grief well-earned,
The King of all exiled,
The staff of faithful souls
Become the laughing-stock
Of heathen men.
... Whoe'er is signed
With the symbol of the faith,
Look with a mourning heart on the Cross of Christ.
Leave Babylon behind,
Fight for the Kingdom of God,
For the water of life
Fight.

More Latin Lyrics

58 HE THAT HATH AN EAR ...
(Rev. 2.7)

There is a mosque in a Mohammedan village and over the door a half-worn inscription – 'I am the bread of life' – the only thing that remains to show that Christ was once worshipped there and not Mohammed. For what became of those seven churches in Asia Minor to which John wrote those gracious letters of warning and encouragement, of threatening and hope? The threat has been fulfilled – but not the hope. Ephesus, to whom Paul wrote one of his greatest epistles, to which Timothy himself had ministered, Ephesus was not found faithful – and in a few centuries Christ was dethroned to make room for Mohammed, and the crescent shone instead of the cross over the church that had surpassed Diana's temple. Ephesus, Smyrna, Pergamos, Thyatira, Sardis, Laodicea. These were the seven golden candlesticks – and with the single exception of Philadelphia, over against them is written – 'Their lamps are gone out.'

Truly, it was not only for the benefit of his immediate audience that Christ told a story about a vineyard and its unfaithful tenants. 'I say unto you, the Kingdom shall be taken from you, and given unto a nation bringing forth the fruits thereof.' 'The Kingdom', says Alexander Maclaren, 'has been taken from the churches of Asia Minor, Africa and Syria, because they bore no fruit. It is not held by us under other conditions.'

May it not be, that in this tremendous challenge of the non-Christian religions, there is the same warning that once was sent from Patmos. Materialism, not Mohammedanism, is upon us like a sea – 'the hour of temptation' – that was to try them is come upon us too. And in that hour of temptation there was one church of all the seven that kept her troth, the only church of all the seven that stands firm to this day – because she had the courage to find in the path of obedience 'the way of escape'. 'Behold,' said Christ to the church in Philadelphia, 'I have set before thee an open door.' 'Behold,' says Christ to the church in Christendom, 'I have set before thee an open world.' 'And I that speak' – here is the promise – 'am He that openeth – and no man shutteth.' 'And I that speak' – here is the threat – 'am He that shutteth, and no man openeth.'

97

Which, being translated, is the concluding paragaph of Dr Mott's Report:

> For the Church not to rise to the present situation and meet the present opportunity will result in hardening the minds and hearts of its members, and making them unresponsive to God. If the situation now confronting the Church throughout the world does not move to larger consecration and prompt and aggressive effort, it is difficult to imagine what more God could do to move the Church, unless it be to bring upon it some great calamity.... The only thing which will save the Church from the imminent perils of growing luxury and *materialism* is the putting forth of all its powers on behalf of the world without Christ. Times of material prosperity have ever been the times of greatest danger to Christianity. The Church needs a supreme world-purpose, a gigantic task, something which will call out all its energies, something too great for man to accomplish, and therefore something which will throw the Church back upon God himself.

Back upon God himself – there after all is the conclusion of the whole matter – the explanation of our failure – in that we have gone from him – the assurance of our victory – in that we are going back – and going back the stronger for our defeat. It was not for nothing that Christ once left his disciples to a task that was too hard for them, and kept out of the way until they had spent their strength for nought, and came to him in desperation. And, when he had performed what he said himself was the hardest miracle, they asked him, 'Master, why could not we cast him out?', and he answered, 'Because of your unbelief.' Paul himself had to come the same road – 'By my own self' he writes, speaking of a great emergency that had fallen upon him – 'By my own self, I was already doomed to death – that I might rely no more upon myself, but upon God.' And so this crisis has come upon us just when our vitality seemed lowest – crashing down the barriers of our indifference and our complacency, to make room for the strength of God. The Church counted up in careful paragraphs what she was pleased to call her '*practical* resources' – her men and her money, and her prestige; and God has let her drain them to the very dregs, to teach her that her first and greatest 'practical resource' is Himself. 'Let him take hold of My strength' – and *then* – 'Go – in *this* thy might.' 'We stand paralysed in the presence of evil,' says Dr Oldham, 'because we have lost the sense of God. Where a man has the conviction of God upon him – *there* is power.'

To the Christian Union (unpublished)

59 A FORM OF GODLINESS
(2 Tim. 3.5)

This is the reason why the Church's appeal carries so little conviction with it — that there is so little conviction behind it. *We do not believe the things that we pretend to believe* — if we did, the power of the Church would be limited only by the power of God. God's omnipotence is round us like a sea — but some of us, says Maclaren drily 'seem cased in waterproof'. And this is why we stand shamefaced and tongue-tied in the presence of the Philistines, and this is what gives the sting to their mocking. We know our weaknesses better than they do. For if it is hard to give a reason for the faith that is in you, it is a good deal harder to give a reason for the faith that *isn't* in you — and that is what we have been trying to do. It has been an ignominious and a dismal failure; but the very shame of it will be our salvation.

What was wrong with us was not that we needed a new Christianity, but that we needed a new realization of Christianity. We folded our hands and said in a pious exaltation — 'This is the mystery that overcometh the world, even our faith' — and were grievously surprised to find that *our* faith was not the type that would overcome anything, let alone the world. 'Other men laboured, and we entered into their labours.' No wonder that Paul's temper rose at the puerilities of such as we — 'By the time that ye ought to be teachers,' he said in disgust, 'ye have need to be taught the first principles. . . . Be *men* in understanding, and not babes.' We have brought the dignity of our religion into contempt with our impertinences. It is ourselves we have to thank for the impression that it implies higher mental calibre to be an agnostic than to be a Christian, that Christianity is too easy a solution for the 'burden of the mystery of all this unintelligible world'. It is our own miserable shamefacedness, our pitiful apologetic attitude towards the greatest thing in the world, that has made a man proud to say 'I am an Agnostic', and ashamed to say 'I am a Christian'. And this is the reason why so many have turned back and walked no more with Him — not as in old Judea because the ideal that Christ had set before them was too high — but because the ideal that we have set before them was too low. We have cheapened Him — not only in our living, but in our speech of Him. It was the cheapness of our religion that has brought about the cheapness of our life.

'I am not ashamed of the Gospel of Christ,' said Paul, 'because it is the power of God unto salvation.' There was some excuse for Paul's magnificent defiance − for Paul's idea of salvation is not ours. It was something more to him than final safety − the evading of the wrath of God − the getting of our miserable souls into heaven at the least possible cost. Salvation to Paul was salvation − and not salvage. 'Being reconciled to God by the death of His Son, we are *saved by sharing in His life*' − sharing in the life of God.

To the Christian Union (unpublished)

Part Five

I WILL ALLURE
AND BRING INTO
THE WILDERNESS

'Behold, I will allure her,
and bring her into the wilderness,
and speak comfortably unto her.'

Hos. 2.14

60 THE DAYS OF OLD
(*Ps. 77.5*)

PAULINUS OF NOLA

Not that they beggared be in mind, or brutes,
That they have chosen their dwelling place afar
In lonely places: but their eyes are turned
To the high stars, the very deep of Truth.
Freedom they seek, an emptiness apart
From worthless hopes, din of the marketplace,
And all the noisy crowding up of things,
And whatsoever wars on the divine,
At Christ's command and for His love, they hate;
By faith and hope they follow after God,
And know their quest shall not be desperate,
If but the Present conquer not their souls
With hollow things: that which they see they spurn
That they may come at what they do not see,
Their senses kindled like a torch, that may
Blaze through the secrets of eternity.
The transient's open, everlastingness
Denied our sight; yet still by hope we follow
The vision that our minds have seen, despising
The shows and forms of things, the loveliness
Soliciting for ill our mortal eyes.
The present's nothing: but eternity
Abides for those on whom all truth, all good,
Hath shone, in one entire and perfect light.

Mediaeval Latin Lyrics

61 UNDERSTAND WISDOM
(*Prov. 8.5*)

St Antony, called the father of monks and prince of solitaries, declared, 'With our neighbour is life and death.' If then the love of God is best expressed in love of men for God's sake, what was the legacy of the Desert Fathers in their solitude?

One intellectual concept they did give to Europe: eternity. Here again they do not formulate it: they embody it. These men, by the very exaggeration of their lives, stamped infinity on the imagination of the West. They saw the life of the body as Paulinus saw it, '*occidui temporis umbra*', a shadow at sunset. 'The spaces of our human life set over against eternity' – it is the undercurrent of all Antony's thought – 'are most brief and poor.'

> Think you the bargain's hard, to have exchanged
> The transient for the eternal, to have sold
> Earth to buy heaven?

Twelve centuries later, Donne could pray to be delivered from thinking

> that this earth
> Is only for our prison fram'd,
> Or that Thou'rt covetous
> To them whom Thou lovest, or that they are maim'd
> From reaching this world's sweet who seek Thee thus.

It is the rich compromise of seventeenth-century humanism. But for the fourth century the Kingdom of God was still the pearl of great price hidden in a field, for which a man must sell all that he had if he would buy that field. Paganism was daylight, Augustine's 'queen light', sovereign of the senses, rich in its acceptance of the daylight earth: but Christianity came first to the world as a starlit darkness, into which a man steps and comes suddenly aware of a whole universe, except that part of it which is beneath his feet.

> If Light can thus conceal, wherefore not Life?

Experience was to bring compromise, the alternation of day and night, the *vita mixta* of action and contemplation, 'wherein,' says Augustine, 'the love of truth doth ask a holy quiet, and the necessity of love doth accept a righteous busyness.' But the Desert Fathers knew no compromise. They have no place among the doctors: they have no great place among even the obscurer saints. But the extravagance of their lives is the extravagance of poetry.

> ... *nel mondo ad ora ad ora*
> *m'insegnavate come l'uom s'eterna:*

in the world, hour by hour, they taught us how man makes himself eternal. Starved and scurvy-ridden as the first voyagers across the Atlantic, these finished with bright day and chose the dark.

The Desert Fathers

62 TEMPTATION IN THE WILDERNESS
(*Heb. 3.8*)

The Desert, though it praised austerity, reckoned it among the rudiments of holy living, and not as an end in itself: asceticism had not travelled far from the *ascesis*, the training of the athlete, and the Fathers themselves to their contemporary biographers are the *athletae Dei*, the athletes of God. Human passion, the passion of anger as well as of lust, entangled the life of the spirit: therefore passion must be dug out by the roots. 'Our mind is hampered and called back from the contemplation of God, because we are led into captivity to the passions of the flesh.' The actual words were spoken by the abbot Theonas, but they echo sentence after sentence from Socrates in the *Phaedo*. 'Spirit must brand the flesh that it may live,' said George Meredith, who was no Puritan: and Dorotheus the Theban put it more bluntly fifteen hundred years earlier: 'I kill my body, for it kills me.' Moreover, the wisest of the Fathers discountenanced publicity, dissembling both their moments of ecstasy and the meagreness of their fare. The great Macarius, indeed, seems to have been moved for a while by the ill spirit of competition. Did he hear that one Father ate only a pound of bread, himself was content to nibble a handful of crusts: did another eat no cooked food for the forty

105

days of Lent, raw herbs became his diet for seven years. The fame of the high austerity of Tabenna reached him in his fastness: he came fifteen days' journey across the desert, disguised as a working man, interviewed the abbot, the great and gentle Pachomius, and was admitted on probation with some ado, for he was an old man, said the abbot, and not inured to abstinence like his own monks, who had been trained to it, and would only end by going away with a grievance and an ill word of the monastery. Lent was about to begin: and having observed with an attentive eye the various activities of the brethren, how one brother chose to fast till vespers, another for two days, another for five, how one stood up all night and sat weaving his mats all day, Macarius proceeded to combine these excellences in one person. Providing himself with plenty of palm-fibre steeped and ready for plaiting, he stood himself in a corner for the forty days till Easter, neither eating bread nor drinking water, nor kneeling nor lying, nor sleeping nor speaking, but silently praying and efficiently plaiting, and, to avoid ostentation, eating a few raw cabbage leaves on Sundays. The infuriated brethren came seething about their abbot – it would seem that Pachomius had been disappointingly unaware of the record performance being given in their midst – demanding where he had found this creature without human flesh who was bringing them all into contempt: either he left, or they did, in one body, that same day. Pachomius heard them out: he meditated, prayerfully, and the identity of his embarrassing visitor was suddenly revealed to him. He went to find him, led him by the hand to his private oratory, and there kissed him and greeted him by name, gently reproaching him for his efforts at disguise from one who had for many years desired to see him. 'I give thee thanks that thou hast clouted the ears of these youngsters of mine [*quia colaphos nostris infantibus dedisti*], and put the conceit out of them. Now, therefore, return to the place from whence thou camest: we have all been sufficiently edified by thee: and pray for us.' Had I been in Macarius' shoes, said the abbé Bremond, I think I would have come out of that church less triumphant than I went in. The Desert was a school of high diplomacy as well as of devotion: and the *Verba Seniorum* has something of the irony of the Gospels.

The Desert Fathers

63 TAKE MY YOKE UPON YOU
(*Matt. 11.29*)

For the ascetic and mystic, a swift translation to eternity and the passing of youth in the denial of youth, must seem great gain. Yet Macarius, inured as he was to abnegation and silence, is shaken by two brothers: they died young. When other of the Fathers would come to see the abbot Macarius, he would take them into their cell, saying, 'Come, see the place of martyrdom of these lesser pilgrims.'

Now, that it should be so is perhaps the ultimate proof of the power of matter, the depth of the warfare between the spirit and the flesh. For the martyr's grave of these lesser pilgrims is not the only waste of youth in human experience. Leaving aside the annihilation of an entire generation in four years, not yet a quarter of a century ago, how many have died or been maimed in chemical and biological research: how many litter the track to the Northern or Southern Pole: how many have been taken by Everest and his peers: how many dead and still to die in the conquest of the air, or in that last exploration which gives this generation its nearest approach to religious ecstasy, the annihilation of space in speed? Gaugin, like any Desert fanatic, left his Paris banking house and his comfortable wife, and watched his small son starve and himself died in nakedness and ecstasy, because he had discovered paint as the Desert discovered God. Van Gogh went mad in struggling to paint light: they found a fragment of a letter in his pocket after he had shot himself. 'Well, my own work, I am risking my life for it, and my reason has half foundered in it – that's all right.' It is not that these are not grieved for: but they are not grudged. No generous spirit will shirk the arduous, provided it be unknown. A man must follow his star. We do not grudge it that these should have left wife and children and lands and reason for the flick of a needle on the speedometer or 'a still life of a pair of old shoes'. The only field of research in which a man may make no sacrifices, under pain of being called a fanatic, is God.

The Desert Fathers

64 WISDOM EXCELLETH FOLLY
(*Eccles. 2.13*)

At one time certain brethren went forth from their monastery to visit the Fathers who dwelt in the desert. And on their coming to a certain aged hermit, he welcomed them with great joy and as the custom is, set a little meal before them. For he saw that they were tired after their journey, and so he made them eat before the ninth hour, and whatever he had in his cell he set down for them to eat, and made much of them. And when evening was come, they recited the customary prayers and psalms, and at night they did likewise. Now the old man was lying quiet by himself in a place apart, and he heard them talking among themselves and saying: 'These hermits keep a better and more plentiful table than we who live in monasteries.' And the old man heard it and held his peace. And when day broke, they took the road to visit another hermit, who lived in the neighbourhood of the old man. But as they were going out the old man said to them: 'Greet him from me and say to him, "Be careful not to water the vegetables."' So when they came to the other old man, they gave him the message. And he understood the reason of it, and kept the brothers with him, and gave them baskets to weave, himself sitting with them, and working without a pause. When evening was come at the lighting of the lamps he added others to the wonted psalms, and when prayers were ended he said to them: 'It is indeed not our custom to eat every day, but since you have come we must make a feast today': and he set dry bread before them, and salt, saying, 'On your account we must make better cheer,' and he set out a little vinegar and salt and a trifle of oil: and when they had risen from table, he again began upon the psalter till it was close on dawn: and he said to them: 'Since you are here, we cannot sing the whole canon, because you must rest a little, being weary from your journey.' When morning had come, they would fain have left him at Prime, but the old man would not suffer it, saying: 'Rather must you order it to stay with us several days: I shall not let you go to-day, but for love's sake keep you another three.' And when they heard that, they rose by night and they stole away from that place before the day would break.

The Desert Fathers

65 LET BROTHERLY LOVE CONTINUE
(*Heb. 13.1*)

CYRENAICA IN THE FIFTH CENTURY

The original of this fragment of a desert pilgrimage is in the *Dialogi* of Sulpicius Severus of Toulouse, written on the eve of the barbarian invasion, in the year when France was being stripped of the regions for the defence of Italy.

> Naught but the terror of the Roman name
> Defends the open frontier:
> Tonight there is no watch upon the Rhine.

Yet there is no more premonition of disaster in the proud security of Claudian's verse, than in this quiet prose.

The middle-aged writer of it was to live through the Vandal invasion of 405–6 and died at Marseilles in 410, the year that the Goths under Alaric entered Rome. With his elder contemporary, Ausonius of Bordeaux, Sulpicius Severus represents the first achievement in letters of that *haute bourgeoisie* which has made France the second *patria* of civilized men: but unlike Ausonius, he had abandoned great possessions and a brilliant career at the bar, to follow, in St Jerome's phrase, 'naked, the naked Christ'. He came of good stock of Aquitaine, married into a consular family, and wealth flowed to him from both: but in the spring tides of success, he came under the spell of 'Martin' as he plainly called him, ex-soldier of the Legion, and destined as St Martin of Tours, to rival even St Denys in the heart, though not on the banners of France. After that, as Paulinus of Nola once wrote to him, no voices could call him back 'to that easy spacious road. . . .' 'Preferring the preaching of the fishermen to the prose of Cicero, aye, and your own, you took refuge in the silence of devotion'. Yet a silence not wholly unbroken. Though only a few pages remain there is enough to show the first clear spring of Gallic prose, subtle, ironic and humane.

We had arranged to meet, my friend Gallus and I: he is very dear to me, not only for his own qualities, but for the sake of Martin's

109

memory: he had been his disciple as I was. And as we talked, who should come upon us but my friend Postumianus back from the East, whither he had gone from his own country three years ago. I held him, this man so dear to me, in my arms. We stood gazing at each other, blockishly, and wept for very joy, and gazed again, walking and stopping, till at last we flung our cloaks upon the ground and sat down together.

(continued below)

66 WE TOOK SWEET COUNSEL TOGETHER
(*Ps. 55.14*)

Postumianus fixed his eyes on me: he was the first to speak.

It is three years, Sulpicius, since I said goodbye to you and left this place. Our course was set for Alexandria, but a southerly wind fought us back, and our wary seamen dropped anchor and let the ship ride. Before our eyes stretched the unbroken line of coast: we set out for it in skiffs and, stepping ashore, looked on a country empty of any trace of human toil or habitation. About a mile from the beach I spied a little hut amid the sands, its roof like the keel of a ship. I made my way towards it and found an old man clad in skins turning a grindstone with his hand. I greeted him, and he made me benignly welcome. We told him that we had come ashore to see what kind of place it was, and what manner of man its inhabitants might be: that we were Christians, and above all would seek to know if there were Christian men amid these solitudes.

Then indeed, weeping for joy, he cast himself at our feet: again and again he embraced us and would have us pray with him: then, strewing sheepskins on the ground, made us sit down, and set before us a truly sumptuous meal, not less than half a loaf of barley bread. There were four of us, himself the fifth. He also brought a bunch of herbs, bushy in leaf like mint, and a taste like honey, extraordinarily delicate and sweet: we were delighted with it and ate it till we could eat no more.

At that, I glanced smiling at my friend Gallus. 'What about it, Gallus? What think you of that for a feast, a bunch of herbs and half a loaf among five men?' Gallus reddened a little at my teasing, for he is a sensitive soul. 'Sulpicius, you never let a chance go of poking fun at my greed. But it is inhumane to force us Gallic men to live as the angels do – though I think myself that the angels eat for the sheer pleasure of eating: and I should think very little of that barley loaf even if I had it to myself.'

After this, I pass over that Cyrenian feast, or Gallus will think we are talking at him – we were with our host for a week. Well, next day when some of the neighbours began drifting in to see us, we found out what our host had taken great pains to keep from us, that he was a priest. Then we went with him to the church, about a mile away, but shut out of sight by the bulk of a mountain. It was thatched with brushwood, not much more ambitious than our host's habitation, where a man could not stand without stooping. This moved us above all, that nothing among them is bought or sold. What fraud or theft may be they know not. Gold and silver they have not, nor desire to have: when I tried to offer the priest ten gold pieces, he shrank away, protesting in his nobler wisdom: 'The church is not builded by gold but rather destroyed by it.' For affection's sake, we urged on him a garment or so, and he accepted them. By this time the sailors were shouting to us to come aboard, and we took our departure.

Queen Mary's Book for India

67 BE NOT AFRAID, YE BEASTS OF THE FIELD
(*Joel 2.22*)

'Marvellous are the condescensions of the grace of God . . . yet how befitting His loving-kindness that those who have renounced all fellowship and service of men . . . should themselves receive the good offices of dumb beasts and a kind of human ministering.' Yet the Saints have had no monopoly of the kindness that is between men and beasts. Homer pitied the crying of the sea-birds when

111

the village folk have stolen their unfledged young from the nest: and old Argos on the dunghill, full of fleas, wagging his tail and dropping his ears at the sound of Odysseus' voice, but unable to drag himself nearer for old age, is the most moving thing of its kind in literature. Plutarch was eloquent on the 'native magnanimity' that he found more often in beasts than in mankind: and he is never so engaging as when he describes the elephant that knew itself more stupid than the rest of the troupe, and was found one night rehearsing and 'conning its lessons' by moonlight; or the hedgehog who goes through a vineyard laboriously impaling grapes upon its little spines, till finally, itself a walking bunch of grapes, it bends its steps towards home and the regaling of its family: or the horn-owl who so admires the rhythmic dancing of men that it watches them in an ecstasy, humping its shoulders and jigging on its perch, and lo, the fowler creeps up behind and takes him unawares. It is a hard heart that will not lament him, or that will not contrast 'the lovely friendship and civil society of pismires' with that of politicians. Boethius, himself in prison, wrote half a dozen lines on a wild bird caged in a cellar that sprang too high and saw the waving trees, and how thereafter it spurned its seed and its honeyed drink with small indignant claws.

> And all day long it pines for the green leaves,
> And whispering 'the woods', it grieves — it grieves.

Twelve centuries later Swift opened his cupboard door to put coal on the fire, after Patrick was gone to bed; 'and there I saw in a closet a poor linnet he has bought to bring over to Dingley. . . . I believe he does not know he is a bird: where you put him, there he stands, and seems to have neither hope nor fear.' St Malo would not move his cloak, because a wren had nested in it: and the other day a professional in a golf championship let go his chance of it, because he would not play his ball out of a thrush's nest.

For if the dark places of the earth have always been full of the habitations of cruelty, there has always been a spring of mercy in mankind. The Roman virtue of *pietas* is the strong root from which our pity, in every sense, derives. Religion has had its own savageries: yet even the arbitrary Godhead of the Book of Job was concerned for the young ravens wandering from the nest for lack of meat, and it was Christ's claim that a huddle of feathers on the ground was not unregarded by the Father of mankind. 'With Christ,' said Sulpicius Severus, 'every brute beast is wise, and every savage creature gentle': and St Kevin refused the levelling of the mountains about Glendalough to make his monks rich pasture, because he would not have God's creatures disturbed for him. In the first paradise that lies behind the memory of the world there was no cruelty: and when Isaiah, sick of war, made his poem of the golden world, the climax-vision was a holy mountain where 'they shall not hurt nor destroy.' And whether these ancient ways of thought seem to us only the delusions sloughed by a wiser world, or whether

> those first affections,
> Those shadowy recollections...
> Are still the fountain-light of all our day.
> Are still a master-light of all our seeing

it matters very little.

> For still the heart doth need a language, still
> Doth the old instinct bring back the old names.

The beasts have still their way with us: Dürer's hare looks out on the world with his timid confiding; and the gentlest of the gods still has in his armoury

> a twilight air
> That can make anchorites of kings.

Beasts and Saints

68 DOMINION OVER EVERY LIVING THING
(*Gen. 1.28*)

The most fragrant of these stories, *The Hermit's Garden* and *The Penitent Wolf*, are from a Latin original. They were told to Sulpicius Severus by his friend Postumianus, just off his ship at Narbonne, after three years journeying in North Africa: the two sat together on their cloaks, Postumianus now and then hitching his a little nearer. The *Dialogus* which records that conversation is one of the earliest instances of the idiosyncrasy of French prose, although the words are Latin: and the pages of it are haunted by a gracious ghost, the Abbé Bremond of blessed memory, so near a neighbour in birthplace though so far divided in time, and master, like his predecessor, of a gay and gentle irony. Sulpicius was a barrister of Toulouse, friend and contemporary of St Paulinus of Nola: like him, he was fortunate in birth and ambition and friendship: and like him, renounced the world in his prime. But a kind of exquisite worldliness kept with him, a sidelong glancing wit, and a way of writing prose that runs like water. The *Dialogi* were probably written about 405, a few years before Sulpicius died in 410, the year of the sack of Rome. His friend Paulinus survived him, and Rome, for another twenty years.

THE HERMIT'S GARDEN IN THE DESERT

When I first entered the desert, about twelve miles from the Nile − I had one of the brethren for guide, a man who knew the country well − we came to where an old monk lived at the foot of a mountain. And there, a thing very rare in those parts, was a well. He had an ox, whose sole business it was to draw up the water by turning a wheel: for the well was said to be a thousand or more feet deep. He had a garden too, full of many sorts of vegetables: a thing against nature in the desert, where everything is so parched and burnt by the rays of the sun that it seldom gives root or seed, and then but scant. But the labour that the saint shared with his ox, and his own industry, were to profit: for the constant watering gave such richness to the sand that we saw the herbs growing in the garden, green and lavish. On these the ox lived, together with his master: and from this plenty the good man provided a feast for us as well. I saw then what you men of Gaul will hardly believe, the pot of vegetables that he was preparing for our meal boiling without any fire under it: so great is the heat of the sun that it would cook a Gallic meal as well as any cooks you please.

After supper, as evening drew on, he invited us to a palm tree, the fruit of which he sometimes used; it was about two miles away. For these trees indeed exist in the desert, though not many: and whether it was the skill of the men of old time, or the nature of the soil, begat them, I know not: or else God foreseeing that the desert would some day be inhabited by the saints, prepared them for His servants. For the most part, those who live in these remote solitudes live on the fruit of these trees, since no other succeeds in growing here.

We came then to this tree, led by our kindly host: and there stumbled upon a lion. At sight of him, my guide and I quaked, but the saintly old man went unfalteringly on, and we followed him, timorously enough. The wild beast − you would say it was at the command of God −

modestly withdrew a little way and sat down, while the old man plucked the fruit from the lower branches. He held out his hand, full of dates; and up the creature ran and took them as frankly as any tame animal about the house: and when it had finished eating, it went away. We stood, watching and trembling; reflecting, as well we might, what valour of faith was in him, and what poverty of spirit in us.

Beasts and Saints

69 THE WOLF SHALL DWELL WITH THE LAMB
(*Isa. 11.6*)

Another man, no less remarkable, we saw, living in a poor hut, where only one could enter at a time. The story was told of him that a she-wolf used to stand beside him at his meal, and that never did the creature fail to come at the appointed time, or to wait outside until he offered her whatever bread had been left over from his poor meal: and then she would lick his hand, and as if her task were over and the comfort of her presence duly given, would go away.

But it once so happened that the holy man had gone with a brother who had come to see him, to put him on his way, and was a long time absent, not getting home until nightfall. Meantime the beast had come at the usual meal hour. She felt that her friend and patron was absent, and went into his empty cell, inquisitive to find where its inhabitant might be. By chance a palm-basket with five loaves was hanging within reach: she ventured to take one, devoured it, and then, the crime perpetrated, made off.

The hermit came in, and saw his basket torn: he perceived the damage his household store had suffered, and near the threshold he recognized the crumbs where someone had been eating bread: nor had he much doubt as to the person of the thief. Then as the days went by and the creature did not come – too conscious of her bold act to come to him she had wronged, and affect innocence – the hermit took it sorely to heart that he had lost the company of his pet. At last when the seventh day had gone by, his prayers were answered: there she was, as he sat at his meal,

115

as of old. But it was easy to perceive the embarrassment of the penitent: she stood, not daring to come near, her eyes fixed in profound shame upon the ground, and plainly entreating pardon. Pitying her confusion, the hermit called her to come near, and with a caressing hand he stroked the sad head: and finally, refreshed his penitent with two loaves for one. And she, forgiveness won and her grieving ended, resumed her wonted office. Consider, I pray you, in this example of it the power of Christ, with whom every brute beast is wise, and every savage creature gentle.

Beasts and Saints

70 WOE TO HIM THAT IS ALONE
(*Eccles. 4.10*)

To the Roman civic conscience the exiles in the desert are deserters from a sinking ship, fugitives from a rotting civilisation, concerned only for their personal integrity. Augustine had the civic conscience; the sack of Rome sent him to his book of reconstruction, a city that had foundations, whose builder and maker is God, but a city that could be built on the rubble of the Empire, even as Blake would have built Jerusalem among the dark Satanic mills. 'We are of God,' the Desert seemed to say, 'and the whole world lieth in wickedness.' One of the oldest brief summaries of the Desert rule is the answer of an old man questioned as to what manner of man a monk should be: 'So far as in me is, alone to the alone (*solus ad solum*).' 'Except,' said the abbot Allois, 'a man shall say in his heart, I alone and God are in this world, he shall not find peace.'

Now this – profoundly true of the first encounter of the soul and God, though not of the ultimate adoration that burns up all knowledge of a man's self – is a kind of treason to the *civitas Dei*, nor does it represent the whole of the Desert teaching. 'With our neighbour,' said Antony, prince of solitaries, 'is life and death.' But it has enough truth in it to shadow forth the supreme temptation for the saint, the artist, and the lover, the temptation of the narrow world that has room only for the saint and God, the artist and his subject, the lover and his beloved.

116

Who is so safe as we, where none can do
Treason to us, except one of us two?

Portus impassibilitatis, mansionem in terra quietorum praeparare, the
haven of invulnerable living, to build a house in the land of quiet men,
phrases such as these do but make articulate the sighing of the prisoners
of a clattering world, the last delusion of the human heart that solitude is
peace. Sentence after sentence from the Desert, the 'trackless place' of
Antony's desire, fall on the ear with a dangerous enchantment; the
remoteness of death is in the lovely rhythms of the old hermit's
questioning. 'Tell me, I pray thee, how fares the human race: if new
roofs be risen in the ancient cities: whose empire is it that now sways the
world?' Arsenius came from Theodosius' court and the guardianship of
the young princes to Scete, hungry for a quiet that could not be shaken
even by the rustling of reeds or the voice of a bird. It is the same hunger
that gives a sudden eloquence to a quiet aged monk whom Cassian and
his friend Germanus found sitting in a crowded monastery, a monk that
had been a famous solitary in the desert. The young men asked him how
it came that he had left the higher life for the lower: and the whole
vanished sweetness of the life of quiet is in the old man's reply. He told
them of the first days in the desert when few found their way there: 'the
sparseness of those who at that time dwelt in the desert was gracious to us
as a caress; it lavished liberty upon us, in the far-flowing vastness of that
solitude.' But others came to know the sweetness of the quiet which their
coming destroyed: *coangustata vastiori eremi libertate* (no English word
can give the poignancy of the Latin *angustus*); the vaster freedom of the
desert was cabined, and the fire of divine contemplation grew cold.
Sublimity was gone: let him make up for it by obedience. So the old man
came back from the desert, now a thoroughfare, to submit to the yoke of
his abbot's will and the friction of living among men.

A certain brother while he was in the community was restless and
frequently moved to wrath. And he said within himself, 'I shall go and
live in some place in solitude: and when I have no one to speak to or to
hear, I shall be at peace and this passion of anger will be stilled.' So he
went forth and lived by himself in a cave. One day he filled a jug for
himself with water and set it on the ground, but it happened that it
suddenly overturned. He filled it a second time, and again it overturned:
and he filled it a third time and set it down, and it overturned again. And
in a rage he caught up the jug and broke it. Then when he had come to
himself, he thought how he had been tricked by the spirit of anger and

said, 'Behold, here am I alone, and nevertheless he hath conquered me. I shall return to the community, for in all places there is need for struggle and for patience and above all for the help of God.' And he arose and returned to his place.

The truth is that solitude is the creative condition of genius, religious or secular, and the ultimate sterilising of it. No human soul can for long ignore 'the giant agony of the world' and live, except indeed the mollusc life, a barnacle upon eternity.

The Desert Fathers

71 GUIDED IN THE WILDERNESS
(*Ps. 78.52*)

Paradoxical as it seems, their [the Desert Fathers] denial of the life of earth has been the incalculable enriching of it, and they have affected the consciousness of generations to which they are not even a name. They thought to devaluate time by setting it over against eternity, and instead they have given it an unplumbed depth. It is as though they first conceived of eternity as everlastingness, the production to infinity of a straight line, and in time men came to know it vertical as well as horizontal, and to judge an experience by its quality rather than its duration. The sense of infinity is now in our blood: and even to those of us who see our life as a span long, beginning in the womb and ending in the coffin or a shovelful of grey ash, each moment of it has its eternal freight.

> *Un punto solo m'è maggior letargo* –
> One point of time hath deeper burdened me
> Than all the centuries that have forgot
> How Argo's shadow startled first the sea.

The *saecula sine fine ad requiescendum*, 'the ages of quiet without end,' have been transformed into Boethius' definition of eternity, 'that which encloseth and possesseth the whole fullness of the life everlasting, from which naught of the future is absent, and naught of the past hath flowed away.' Not one of the Desert Fathers could have conceived it: they might even have denied it as a heresy: yet the mind of man moved a stage nearer to it with each moment of their ravaged lives.

The Desert Fathers

Part Six

ONE GENERATION
PASSETH AWAY

'One generation passeth away,
and another generation cometh:
but the earth abideth for ever.'

Eccles. 1.4

72 PEACE AND TRUTH
(*Isa. 39.8*)

ST EPHRAEM

St Ephraem was a lover of quiet, said St Basil, a little, it would seem, like the Venerable Bede, seldom out of his cell, for ever busy with his commentaries, but accessible to any man who came for teaching: with a kind of blessedness about him. To himself, he was a poor-spirited creature, who if he had but to say a word in season to his neighbour, looked forward to it with embarrassment and dread. But it so happened that in his old age there came a cruel famine on the countryside; he saw the peasants dying about him, and their desperation, not his own, drove him out of his cell. He bearded the rich men of Edessa, asking them if they had no pity 'for human nature dying before your eyes,' or would they keep their rotting wealth intact to the final damnation of their souls? They paltered with him: they said that they had no one who could be trusted to lay out the money, for all men traffic for their private gain. 'Ye think so,' said he, 'of me?' And with the money he shamed them into giving, the diffident scholar turned man of affairs, building a rough-and-ready hospital of three hundred beds, nursing and feeding those who had any spark of life in them, burying the dead. Another year came with plentiful harvests, and his salvaged folk went back to their farms, and there was nothing more for them that he could do: and suddenly empty-handed, he went back to his quiet cell and in a month was dead. Winter had indeed come upon him, the 'infinite tempest' had found him, as he thought, naked, and spoiled and come to no perfecting; but to his contemporaries it seemed that God's love had given him, as to his other quiet servant Stephen, a sudden glory at his end. He had seen human nature dying before his eyes: and in succouring it, he was to see the taking of the manhood into God.

PRAYER OF ST EPHRAEM

Have mercy upon me, Thou that alone art without sin, and save me, who alone art pitiful and kind: for beside Thee, the Father most blessed, and Thine only begotten Son who was made flesh for us, and the Holy Ghost who giveth life to all things, I know no other, and believe in no other. And now be mindful of me, Lover of men, and lead me out of the prison-

121

house of my sins, for both are in Thy hand, O Lord, the time that Thou didst will me to come into this world, and the time that Thou shalt bid me go out from it elsewhere. Remember me that am without defence, and save me a sinner: and may Thy grace, that was in this world my aid, my refuge and my glory, gather me under its wings in that great and terrible day. For Thou knowest, Thou who dost try the hearts and reins, that I did shun much of evil and the byways of shame, the vanity of the impertinent and the defence of heresy. And this not of myself, but of Thy grace wherewith my mind was lit. Wherefore, holy Lord, I beseech Thee, bring me into Thy kingdom, and deign to bless me with all that have found grace before Thee, for with Thee is magnificence, adoration, and honour, Father, Son, and Holy Ghost. Amen.

The Desert Fathers

73 NOT PEACE, BUT A SWORD
(*Matt. 10.34*)

PAULINUS OF NOLA

Paulinus, governor of a province and consul before he was thirty, had taken a sudden journey into Spain. He gave no explanation, took leave of no one, not even so much as the *salve* of courteous enemies for which Ausonius pleaded. Love and friend he had put far from him. There followed four years of impenetrable and cruel silence.

Four years is a long time at seventy, and Ausonius loved him. At the end of the four years three letters came to him by a single messenger. Paulinus has chosen. Henceforth his mind is a torch, flaming through the secrets of eternity, but his heart aches for his old master, and the gratitude he lavishes upon him might have deceived most men. It did not deceive Ausonius – 'To Paulinus, when he had answered other things, but had not said that he would come.' There follow pages that have only one parallel, the cry from Po Chu-i in exile, four centuries later – 'O Wei-chih, Wei-chih! This night, this heart. Do you know them or not? Lo Tien bows his head.' Then Ausonius falls to dreaming; he hears the grating of the boat on the beach, the shouting of the people in the street, the footsteps, the familiar knock on the door.

> Is't true? or only true that those who love
> Make for themselves their dreams?

That wounding spearhead of Virgil reached its mark. Paulinus answered in something like an agony of love and compassion. Once again he pleaded the mystery that no man sees from without: then the crying of his own heart silenced the sober elegiacs, and he breaks into one of the loveliest lyric measures of the ancient world.

TO AUSONIUS

> I, through all chances that are given to mortals,
> And through all fates that be,
> So long as this close prison shall contain me,
> Yea, though a world shall sunder me and thee,
>
> Thee shall I hold, in every fibre woven,
> Not with dumb lips, nor with averted face
> Shall I behold thee, in my mind embrace thee,
> Instant and present, thou, in every place.
>
> Yea, when the prison of this flesh is broken,
> And from the earth I shall have gone my way,
> Wheresoe'er in the wide universe I stay me,
> There shall I bear thee, as I do to-day.
>
> Think not the end, that from my body frees me,
> Breaks and unshackles from my love to thee;
> Triumphs the soul above its house in ruin,
> Deathless, begot of immortality.
>
> Still must she keep her senses and affections,
> Hold them as dear as life itself to be.
> Could she choose death, then might she choose forgetting:
> Living, remembering, to eternity.

After this there is silence.

The Wandering Scholars

74 BEHOLD, THOU ART FAIR
(*Song of Sol. 1.15*)

JAMES THE DEACON

That saintly man of God, my own bishop, Nonnus, a man marvellous great and a mighty monk of the monastery called Tabenna, by reason of his rare and gracious way of life, had been reft from the monastery and ordained a bishop. Come together as we were in the afore-named city, the bishop thereof appointed us our lodging in the basilica of the Blessed Julian the Martyr. We entered, and followed to where the other bishops sat, in front of the door of the basilica.

And as we sat, certain of the bishops besought my master Nonnus that they might have some instruction from his lips: and straightway the good bishop began to speak to the weal and health of all that heard him. And as we sat marvelling at the holy learning of him, lo! on a sudden she that was first of the actresses of Antioch passed by: first of the dancers was she, and riding on an ass: and with all fantastic graces did she ride, so decked that naught could be seen upon her but gold and pearls and precious stones: the very nakedness of her feet was hidden under gold and pearls: and with her was a splendid train of young men and maidens clad in robes of price, with torques of gold about their necks. Some went before and some came after her: but of the beauty and the loveliness of her there could be no wearying for a world of men. Passing through our midst, she filled the air with the fragrance of musk and of all scents that are sweetest. And when the bishops saw her so shamelessly ride by, bare of head and shoulder and limb, in pomp so splendid, and not so much as a veil upon her head or about her shoulders, they groaned, and in silence turned away their heads as from great and grievous sin.

But the most blessed Nonnus did long and most intently regard her: and after she had passed by still he gazed and still his eyes went after her. Then, turning his head, he looked upon the bishops sitting round him. 'Did not,' said he, 'the sight of her great beauty delight you?'

They answered him nothing. And he sank his face upon his knees, and the holy book that he held in his good hands, and his tears fell down upon his breast, and sighing heavily he said again to the bishops, 'Did not the sight of her great beauty delight you?'

But again they answered nothing. Then said he, 'Verily, it greatly delighted me, and well pleased was I with her beauty: whom God shall set in presence of His high and terrible seat, in judgment of ourselves and our episcopate.'

And again he spoke to the bishops.

What think you, beloved? How many hours hath this woman spent in her chamber, bathing and adorning herself with all solicitude and all her mind on the stage, that there may be no stain or flaw in all that body's beauty and its wearing, that she may be a joy to all men's eyes, nor disappoint those paltry lovers of hers who are but for a day and to-morrow are not? And we who have in heaven a Father Almighty, an immortal Lover, with the promise of riches eternal and rewards beyond all reckoning, since eye hath not seen nor ear hath heard nor hath it ascended into the heart of man to conceive the things that God hath prepared for them that love Him — but what need is there of further speech? With such a promise, the vision of the Bridegroom, that great and splendid and ineffable face, whereon the Cherubim dare not look, we adorn not, we care not so much as to wash the filth from our miserable souls, but leave them lying in their squalor.

And with that, he laid hold on me, deacon and sinner, and we made our way to this hospice, where a cell had been given us. And going into his own chamber, he flung himself on the paved floor, his face to the ground; and beating his breast he began to weep, saying,

Lord Christ, have mercy on a sinful man and an unworthy, for a single day's adorning of a harlot is far beyond the adorning of my soul. With what countenance shall I look upon Thee? Or with what words shall I justify myself in Thy sight? I shall not hide my heart from Thee, Thou knowest its secrets. Woe is me, worthless and sinful that I am, for I stand at Thy altar, and offer not the fair soul that Thou askest. She hath promised to please men, and hath kept her word: I have promised to please Thee, and through my sloth have lied. Naked am I in heaven and in earth, for I have not done Thy bidding. My hope is not in any good thing that I have done, but my hope is in Thy pity, whereto I trust my salvation.

Such was his prayer and such his lamenting: and vehemently did we keep the feast that day.

The Desert Fathers

75 TO KNOW WISDOM
(*Prov. 1.2*)

Granted Virgil and Ovid, it is in the last three centuries of the Empire, the centuries of which the classical scholar is rightly impatient, that the spiritual foundations of the Middle Ages were laid. It is hardly possible to exaggerate their importance: the centuries of Augustine and Jerome and Ambrose; of the *Confessions,* the *De Civitate Dei,* the Vulgate translation of the Bible, the first of the Latin hymns; the massive strategic common sense of Gregory the Great; the moulding of the Liturgy; the *Te Deum*; the founding of the Benedictine order that kept the gates of knowledge for Europe; the codifying of Roman law; the inspiration of Cassiodorus to 'utilise the vast leisure of the convent' in copying manuscripts. . . . And in the smaller things, they are the centuries of Donatus and Priscian, the schoolmasters of Europe for a thousand years; of Boethius' *Consolation of Philosophy,* written in prison, the book of most serene and kindly wisdom that the Middle Ages knew. In every century men have listened to it, heard in it a kind of angelus rung in the evening of the ancient world. Not Augustine himself breaks his mind upon eternity as Boethius did. . . . It was fortunate for the sanity of the Middle Ages that the man who taught them so much of their philosophy was of a temperament so humane and so serene; that the 'mightiest observer of mighty things,' who defined eternity with an exulting plenitude that no man has approached before or since, had gone to gather violets in a spring wood, and watched with a sore heart a bird in a cage that had caught a glimpse of waving trees, and now grieved its heart out, scattering its seed with small impotent claws:

> This bird was happy once in the high trees.
> You cage it in your cellar, bring it seed,
> Honey to sip, all that its heart can need
> Or human love can think of: till it sees,
> Leaping too high within its narrow room
> The old familiar shadow of the leaves,
> And spurns the seed with tiny desperate claws.
> Naught but the woods despairing pleads,
> The woods, the woods again, it grieves, it grieves.

Dante saw Boethius among the twelve 'living and victorious splendours':

> The body, whence that soul was reft, now lies
> Down in Cieldaro, but the soul from exile
> And martyr's pain hath come unto this peace.

Yet the real achievement is that the soul had come into this peace before it left the body; had endured its travail:

> This discord in the pact of things,
> This endless war 'twixt truth and truth,

and found its reconciliation in what is perhaps the deepest word of mediaeval philosophy or religion, 'simplicitas Dei', the simplicity of God.

The Wandering Scholars

76 PUT YE ON THE LORD JESUS CHRIST
(Rom. 13.14)

In the late summer of 386, Pontician, a distinguished civil servant, came to visit his friends Augustine and Alypius in Milan. He was, like them, from North Africa, and the three sat down to talk. A book lay beside him on a *mensam lusoriam* (as it might be a card-table), and he picked it up, thinking it one of the text-books that Augustine was using in his lectures on rhetoric: it was near the end of term, within three weeks of the holidays for the vintage. The book was the Epistles of St Paul, and the courtly eyebrows lifted, for whatever his personal devotion, he had not associated his friend Augustine with that kind of reading. Augustine protested that he had been spending a good deal of time upon it: and from that Pontician fell to talk of Antony, of whom neither of his friends had ever heard, and from Antony, of that rich solitude of the Desert, to which so many men were now being drawn. He told the story of the codex in the little house outside Trèves, and how sorrowfully he himself had turned his back on it and come away. Augustine sat, knowing that the thing to which he listened was that which he had sought and fled from for twelve years, 'that whereof not the finding but the sole seeking

127

is beyond the treasuries of kings and all this ambient bodily delight.' He sat in silence, and his soul quailed away from it as from death.

Pontician took his leave, and Augustine, starting up with a cry, went from the house out into the garden, to the ultimate agony of the will. They came about him, plucking at him, the trifling, heedless pleasures of his daily use, the dear indulgence of the unthinking flesh: *'And dost thou send us away?'* and *'From this moment we shall never be with thee, to all eternity, any more.'* There came to him the memory of how a single sentence heard one day had sent Antony into poverty and solitude: for he had great possessions. 'Go and sell all that thou hast and give to the poor, and thou shalt have treasure in heaven: and come and follow me.' He came back to the seat in the garden where he had thrown down his St Paul, and opened it at random. '"Not in rioting and drunkenness, not in chambering and wantonness, not in strife and envying: but put ye on the Lord Jesus Christ and make no provision for the flesh to fulfil the lusts thereof." I had no mind to read further; nor was there need.'

Antony had gone to the desert: but there Augustine did not follow him. It was not the inhuman austerities, the demon-haunted vigils, impressive as they were to the grosser imagination of his age, that moved him: it was the secret renunciation, the doctrine of the power of the will. 'Fear not,' Antony had said, 'this goodness as a thing impossible, nor the pursuit of it as something alien, set a great way off: it hangeth on our own arbitrament. For the sake of the Greek learning men go overseas . . . but the city of God hath its foundations in every seat of human habitation . . . the Kingdom of God is within. . . . The goodness that is in us doth ask but the human mind.' It asked and found in Augustine the richest mind in Christendom.

The Desert Fathers

77 THE KINGDOM OF GOD IS WITHIN
(*Luke 17.21*)

ON THE MONASTIC VOCATION   ALCUIN

I was hurrying to meet you, my dear son, and instead of the joy of seeing your face, behold only your letter, and that a sad one, telling me that you are so ill that you have come very near the threshold of our life. My son, whatever powers you have left you, offer them now as a hostage to God. Trust in the Lord Christ, who promised heaven at a single word from a thief: and if his mercy, that can both kill and make alive, wills to bring you back to your old health, be in performance as you are now in will. You have me, for whatever I'm worth, either a faithful standby on that awesome journey, or to counsel you and comfort you in life.

As to what your dearness has asked me about the difference between the two places, the canonical and the monastic, and in which it is better to await the last day: God is everywhere, who considers the quality of one's deservings, rather than one's actual situation: and if you have laboured more under the canon's *orarium* than the cowl in serving God, what is there in the actuality (?) of death to make you fling away the token of your labours? If indeed you are determined, if you live, to serve henceforth in the cowl, then turn your thought that way: there is the advantage of prayer, and the solace and intercession of the brethren, and rest for the body there. But if I speak unadvisedly, you have good counsellors with you, who will advise you to your soul's good: never shall my poor love go from you, and if it does not understand as it should, it will anyhow never cease to long for you. I pray you, let me have word of whatever becomes of your life (an amazing phrase that – and in its very simplicity the assurance of immortality), so that if you go, I may go after you with my tears and my prayers. And may God be pitiful and give you happy days, either in time or in eternity.

(It is a question whether Alcuin ever took monastic vows: and his first letter is to a friend contemplating retreat. He is joyous of the news, and urges the fulfilment of the vow. But remember, says he, that in any place, where a good many men are living together, good and evil are found. But a wise mind keeps its own mastery. There is something royal in men that must choose what to avoid and what to follow: neither to be over-doubtful of a place, nor yet to have confidence in it. If place could help, never had angel fallen from heaven, nor man sinned in Paradise. The Kingdom of God is within. That man who recognizes and fears God present in all places will fear to sin: he has his judge.)

Unpublished typescript

78 MERCY, AND NOT SACRIFICE
(*Matt. 9.13*)

ALCUIN

Somewhere in France Alcuin found a stray monk, escaped from Wulfhard, afterwards bishop of Hereford, 789–96:

I found this stray lamb lost in steep places, and moved by pity I brought it back to our house, and bound up its wounds. I send him back, gentle father, to your care: and I entreat you that you will take him in, kind and familiar, for love of Him who brought us all back, wandering on the cliffs, on his own shoulders. Do not drive him off from you by harshness, whom Christ has brought back to himself by pity – and ran to meet him coming back. If any ill-natured tongue urges you to drive him off, let him, whoever he is, beware lest he be driven away by Him who said 'With what judgement ye judge, ye shall be judged.' If he has sinned ten times, haven't we a hundred times? If he owes an hundred pence, do not we ten thousand talents? But what need have I to urge these things on you, when you know them better and keep them more faithfully that I do. I trust in your goodness. Think that it is I prostrate before your feet, not in body but in soul. So hear my prayer for the love of Him who always hears your own. Blessed are the merciful, for they shall obtain mercy. Live, and be happy, and, sweet friend, remember me.

Unpublished typescript

79 LOVELY IN THEIR LIVES
(*2 Sam. 1.23*)

ALCUIN TO ARNO OF SALZBURG, 798 AD

Would that it might please the lord King to suffer you to winter at St Amand, and so for a little while we might, by Christ's compassion, live under one roof, and break the prophet's bread.

Oh joyous is love, and sweet that presence, and happy that life where that never is absent which ever is beloved. For love that burneth in absence, in presence hath its joy. I grant you that God is everywhere present, yet is it one thing to be perceived as a shadow in a mirror, another to be seen in actual fashion and in presence: whereof the Truth itself saith: 'Blessed are the pure in heart for they shall see God.' So may our heart be cleansed in this far exile that it may see the vision most blessed in our fatherland. Let us use this perishable world in love imperishable, that we may know the fruition of God in glory abiding. Lord Christ, make us love Thee, and hate that of which Thou hast said 'The world hateth me, because it seeth Him not neither knoweth Him.'

O King of glory and Lord of Valours, our warrior and our peace, who hast said 'Be of good cheer, I have overcome the world', be Thou victorious in us Thy servants, for without Thee we can do nothing. Give us to will and to perform. Grant Thy compassion to go before us, Thy compassion to come behind us: before us in our undertaking, behind us in our ending. And what shall I now say, unless that Thy will be done, Who dost will that all men should be saved. Thy will is our salvation, our glory, and our joy.

In some sudden outgoing of my spirit, my brother, I have spoken thus, not orderly as the narrow bounds of a letter demand, but passionately as the stirring of one's heart exacts. Yet do thou, my father and my familiar friend, have patience with the crying of that heart, and hide in thy heart what thou hast heard from mine. Who knows, unless He who knoweth all things, if it will be given me to write to thee to-morrow, or if after to-morrow we shall ever hold sweet converse again? His mercy has given me this day's space, who has given me all I have. And I could not hold my peace, for I know not what the coming day may bring.

But do thou, my brother that art one in soul with me, keep the days of eternity for ever in thy mind: and run with patience along that road which Christ doth show to thee. Let Him be meat and drink to thee, and love and glory. Let not thy heart be shaken by earthly ambition, by the officiousness of flatterers, by the specious face of vanity, by fear of great men, or threat of cruel men, but build thy house upon a rock where no storm can hurt thee. Stand thou intrepid there, despising the tongues of men that slander thee, indifferent to the face of them that praise thee.

And be mindful to help me, thy fellow, with thy holy prayers, that the Saviour of all men may deign in the wideness of his mercy to save me, sunken with the wounding of my many sins, and give me an abiding place in blessedness, though it be on the uttermost bound, with thee, my father, my brother, and my son.

More Latin Lyrics

80 THE CONCORD OF BROTHERS
(*Ecclus. 25.2*)

ALCUIN TO ARNO OF SALZBURG

No mountain and no forest, land nor sea,
Shall block love's road, deny the way to thee...
Yet why must love that's sweet
So bitter tears beget,
Honey and gall in one same goblet set?
Even so, O world, the feet
Of sorrow follow hard upon delight,
Joy breaketh in a cry,
And all sweet things are changed to bitterness.
They will not stay for me: yea, all things haste to die.

Wherefore, O world,
So soon to die,
From us depart,
And thou, my heart,
Make haste to fly
Where is delight that fades not,
The unchanging shore,
The happy house where friend from friend divides not,
And what he loves, he hath for evermore.
Take me, beloved, in thy prayer with thee,
Where shall be no estranging thee and me.

Amor is friendship to Alcuin, as to all the earlier Middle Age, and his loveliest lyric is his song to the cuckoo, the lament for his vanished scholar. It was
in Touraine, the abbey that he had made the most famous school of
manuscript, out of Ireland, in Europe, that Alcuin died. The lament that his
scholar Fredegis wrote for him and his cell left empty, has the silvered light
of the Loire, the faint and exquisite landscapes of Ronsard and Du Bellay:

O little house, O dear and sweet my dwelling,
O little house, for ever fare thee well.
The trees stand round thee with their sighing branches,
A little flowering wood for ever fair.

The Wandering Scholars

81 SHALL THE DUST PRAISE THEE?
(Ps. 30.9)

HIS EPITAPH   ALCUIN

Here halt, I pray you, make a little stay,
O wayfarer, to read what I have writ,
And know by my fate what thy fate shall be.
What thou art now, wayfarer, world-renowned,
I was: what I am now, so shall thou be.
The world's delight I followed with a heart
Unsatisfied: ashes am I, and dust.

Wherefore bethink thee rather of thy soul
Than of thy flesh; — this dieth, that abides.
Dost thou make wide thy fields? in this small house
Peace holds me now: no greater house for thee.
Wouldst have thy body clothed in royal red?
The worm is hungry for that body's meat.
Even as the flowers die in a cruel wind,
Even so, O flesh, shall perish all thy pride.

Now in thy turn, wayfarer, for this song
That I have made for thee, I pray you, say:
'Lord Christ, have mercy on Thy servant here,'
And may no hand disturb this sepulchre,
Until the trumpet rings from heaven's height,
'O thou that liest in the dust, arise,
The Judge of the unnumbered hosts is here!'

Alcuin was my name: learning I loved.
O thou that readest this, pray for my soul.

Here lieth the Lord Abbot Alcuin of blessed memory, who died in peace on the nineteenth of May. And when ye have read this, do ye all pray for him and say, 'May the Lord give him eternal rest.' Amen.

Mediaeval Latin Lyrics

82 THEIR SOUL SHALL BE AS A
WATERED GARDEN
(Jer. 31.12)

WALAFRID STRABO

Walafrid Strabo came from Reichenau and was bitterly cold, and woefully homesick. He wrote in sapphics; three centuries later another scholar will be hankering after his happy valley, this time in rhyme, but the heartache is the same, and the doubt if scholarship is worth the exile. It was, to Walafrid; his Gloss on Holy Writ, a kind of biblical encyclopedia, was one of the few mediaeval books which the Renaissance thought it worth while to print; it went into fresh editions, even in the seventeenth century. But the work that keeps his memory green is not the *Glossa Ordinaria*, but the garden that he made in the wilderness of academic verse, his plot of ground at Reichenau, of sage and rue and southern-wood, poppy and penny-royal, mint and parsley and radishes, and, for love's sake only, gladioli and lilies and roses, even though only plain German roses, no Tyrian purple nor the scarlet splendour of France. Like Johnny Crow, the abbot of Reichenau did dig and sow till he made a little garden; he tells us all about it, from the very beginning; how the nettles were everywhere, and how weeds link up underground; how his seeds, a tiny crop, sprang up, and how he watered them very carefully, sprinkling with his hands, it being dangerous to water from a bucket, by reason of its fierce impetus. The spring showers were gracious, and the moon was tender to it; but bright Phoebus in his strength was too much for some of the weaklings, and they died. He grew ambrosia, but whether this was the ambrosia of the old gods he knows not, and even though it is a vanity it pleases him to look upon his poppies and remember that when Ceres sought Persephone and found her not, they had given her a brief oblivion of her pain. History has been very tender to the stooping figure with the watering pot, and in one poem that figure straightens itself with an undreamt-of dignity.

> When the moon's splendour shines in naked heaven,
> Stand thou and gaze beneath the open sky.
> See how that radiance from her lamp is riven,
> And in one splendour foldeth gloriously

134

Two that have loved, and now divided far,
Bound by love's bond, in heart together are.

What though thy lover's eyes in vain desire thee,
Seek for love's face, and find that face denied?
Let that light be between us for a token;
Take this poor verse that love and faith inscribe.
Love, art thou true? and fast love's chain about thee?
Then for all time, O love, God give thee joy!

The Wandering Scholars

83 THEY SHALL BE FILLED
(*Matt. 5.6*)

RADBOD

In the year of the Incarnation of our Lord 900 there appeared a marvellous sign in heaven. For the stars were seen to flow from the very height of heaven to the lowest horizon, wellnigh as though they crashed one upon the other. And upon this marvel followed woeful calamities, such as a most notable untowardness of the seasons and frequent tempests, rivers also overflowing their banks as in dread likeness of the Deluge and (what was yet more pestilent than these) ominous upheavals of men boasting themselves against God. In this same year, ere the intercalary days were ended, Fulk the archbishop of Rheims and the king Zvendibold were slain, and not many days before, I, Radbod the sinner, was judged worthy to be enrolled among the servants of the holy church of Utrecht: and O would that I be found worthy of that same company in the life eternal. This then shall be my epitaph:

'Hunger and thirst, O Christ, for sight of Thee,
Came between me and all the feasts of earth.
Give Thou Thyself the Bread, Thyself the Wine,
Thou, sole provision for the unknown way.
Long hunger wasted the world wanderer,
With sight of Thee may he be satisfied.'

135

He died, joyous and innocent as he had lived, with the *Laude* of his own antiphon in praise of Blessed Martin upon his lips.

Mediaeval Latin Lyrics

84 JEALOUS FOR JERUSALEM
(*Zech. 1.14*)

Saint Peter Damian is hot against the monks who challenge the grammarians at their own idle game, and bandy vanities with the seculars as if it were the din of a fair, but Damian himself was in his youth a passionate classicist.

Once was Cicero music in my ears, the songs of the poets beguiled me, the philosophers shone upon me with their golden phrases, the sirens enchanted my soul nigh unto death. The Law and the Prophets, Gospel and Epistle, the whole glorious speech of Christ and His servants, seemed to me a poor thing and empty. I know not what the son of Jesse whispered in my ear, so gracious in its consonance of speech and thought, that all these others whom I once had loved fell inarticulate and silent.

Not wholly inarticulate: the haunting rhythms of his own prose betray his debt. '*Caligaverunt in mortem oculi sui, et illa luminaria quae illuminant orbem ad horam extincta sunt.*' 'Darkened in death his eyes, and those lights which lighten the earth at that hour went out.' The mysticism of the twelfth century is in his sermons − on the reticence of Holy Writ, wherein 'silence itself cries out that some greatness is nigh' − and he has what the twelfth century mystics had not, a style that has the plangent resonance of the violin. There are moments when the bow scrapes wildly across the strings, and when the terrific invective that descends like another fiery hail on the sin of the cities of the Plain falls equally upon his unlucky travelling companion, the poor bishop who sat up in the inn playing chess while Damian was at his prayers, the effect is purely comical. But some divinity hedges him. They could nickname that other accuser of the brethren at Geneva 'The Accusative Case', but for Damian there is his own lightning-flash on Hildebrand, 'My holy

Satan'. The aura about him is of a man 'surer of eternity than time'; with all his denunciation of man's flesh, he loses himself, unlike St Bernard, in an *O altitudo*! before the high aspiring of his mind. 'How strange a thing is man! But half a cubit of him, and a universe full of material things will not satisfy it.' It is not the man whose senses are blunt who makes the sternest ascetic, and a great lover wrote the passionate strophes of his sequence on the Song of Songs –

> Who is this
> That knockest at the gate,
> Breaking the sleep of the night?
> That crieth
> O of all virgins fairest,
> Sister, bride,
> Gem that is rarest.
> Rise, O rise,
> Open, sweetest.

But it is in his most famous poem,

> Ad perennis vitae fontem,

that the long struggle of his soul is laid bare. It is by its satisfactions that one judges a soul, and there are stanzas in the *Paradise* that have an echo in Walton's great sentence on Donne, 'His mind was liberal and unwearied in the search of knowledge, with which his vigorous soul is now satisfied.'

> For the fount of life undying
> Once the parched mind did thirst,
> Cramped within its carnal prison,
> Sought the soul its bonds to burst.
> Struggling, gliding, soaring free,
> Comes back the exile to its own country.
>
> Cleansed from all its dregs, the body
> With the spirit knows no war,
> For the mind and flesh made spirit
> One in thought and feeling are.
> Deep their peace and their enjoying,
> From all shame and scandal far.

All the contrary desires of the poets are here: Wyatt's

137

> Nothing on earth more do I crave
> Save that I have, to have it still.

Shelley's

> Thou lovest — but ne'er knew love's sad satiety.
>
> — *Avidi et semper pleni quod habent desiderant.*
>
> What they have they still desire,
> Eager, and yet satisfied:

Shakespeare's

> Wishing me like to one more rich in hope,
> Featured like him, like him with friends possessed,
> Desiring this man's art and that man's scope,
>
> — *Licet cuiquam sit diversum pro labore meritum*
> *Caritas hoc facit suum, quod amat in altero.*
> *Proprium sit singulorum fit commune omnium.*
>
> Let there be a different guerdon
> Unto each man for his pain,
> That which I loved in another
> Love hath brought to me again;
> Thine and mine in full possession,
> Yet 'tis common unto men:

Milton's longing for something fixed where all is moving 'in all the changes of that which is called fortune from without, or the wily subtleties and refluxes of man's thought from within' —

> — *Hinc perenne tenent esse, nam transire transiit.*

Damian is the greatest name in the century.

The Wandering Scholars

138

85 I HAVE CALLED, AND YE REFUSED
(*Prov. 1.24*)

'I tell you, Bernard, the thing is impossible.'

Bernard of Clairvaux looked tranquilly down at Gilles. 'With God all things are possible.'

'Amen,' said Gilles. 'But by your leave, Bernard, you and He are not yet identical.'

The eyes, deep set in the ravaged face, lit up with a smile of extraordinary charm.

'Thank God,' said Gilles, 'you can still laugh. Even at yourself. And if you smile like that at young Robert, he will eat out of your hand all the way back to Clairvaux. But I doubt if you will keep him, once you have him.'

'I shall keep him,' said Bernard. His lips set.

'And your warrant?'

'*Those that Thou gavest me I have kept, and not one of them is lost, save the son of perdition.* And, please God, Robert shall not be that.'

'I do not imagine,' said Gilles soberly, 'that it pleased Him to lose Judas. But He lost him. Has it never struck you, Bernard, that God has more respect for the free will of the creature He made in His own image than you have?'

'It was free will that damned us,' said Bernard.

'That,' said Gilles, 'is not the point.'

Bernard moved impatiently. 'I have no logic, Gilles,' he began, 'and beside you I am an ignorant man. All I know is that if a man has once seen the face of God, as young Robert did, and then turns from it, it were better for him that he had never been born; for he has crucified the Son of God afresh, and put Him to an open shame. And I have vowed not to break my fast till I have seen him face to face, and pleaded with him, on my knees, to come back. And his penance I shall share with him myself.' He was looking straight before him, forgetting to whom he spoke, and the voice that had been harsh and constrained as he began had dropped to a deeper and strangely moving note.

Gilles looked at the young clenched hands, knotted with rheumatism – rheumatism at twenty-six – the thin stooped figure. Did not someone

139

tell him that the Abbot's cell at Clairvaux was so built that he could not stand upright, nor stretch himself out upon his bed?

'If you speak to him like that,' he said gently, 'I think he will come back. But, Bernard,' his eyes had gone to the window beyond which the white pigeons flashed and tumbled in the blue air of May, 'forgive me: are you so sure that to leave Clairvaux, where no man speaks unless in a whisper and the damp drips down the refectory walls and the brethren kneel in green slime on the chapel floor, and to go back to the kind house of Cluny, where he was reared and where his bed if it was hard was dry, is to turn from the face of God, and crucify His Son afresh?'

'I do. If a man puts his hand to the plough and looks back –'

'Bernard,' Gilles's voice was suddenly stern, 'he has turned not from God's face, but from your face. He has not crucified the Son of God afresh, but he is the first deserter from your abbey that was to be the City of God upon earth; and the thing that he has crucified is your pride.'

Peter Abelard

86 THE BLESSINGS OF HEAVEN
(*Gen. 49.25*)

To every man his own eternity. 'Why should it be immense?' said Svidrigailoff in *Crime and Punishment*. 'Why not a small room, a bathroom for instance, with spiders? It would be, if I had my way.'

> Where congregations ne'er break up,
> And Sabbaths never end,

said Dr Watts of his way. To a feebler folk, it is where Dr Johnson folds immutable legs beneath the dinner tables of eternity, and never has his talk out; where the Vapians nightly pass the equinoctial of Quenbus; where Petronius Arbiter cheered his last moments by ordering the breaking of a blue vase which Nero had always hankered after. Petronius writes a really intimate life of that Emperor as the amateur artist, and Anatole France about Petronius: Professor Saintsbury embarks on his *History of Wine* and the 'infinite research involved therein, with a constitution so divinely renewed that he faces with equanimity the drinking of 'more good wine than would now be good for my pocket or perhaps even my health, and more bad than I could contemplate without dismay in my declining years': and meantime pursues left-handedly his translation of the Vulgate *Arthur*: Stevenson writes three more chapters of *Weir of Hermiston*, yet leaves it still a fragment: and Lytton Strachey publishes the *Life and Letters* of Benjamin Jowett, Master of Balliol, with illustrations by Max Beerbohm. It is a good heaven, if a trifle literary. And in one section of it, Kai Lung tells the tale of the peerless princess Taik and the noble minstrel Ch'eng who, to regain her presence, chained his wrist to a passing star and was carried into the Assembly of the Gods.

Review of Kai Lung's Golden House by Ernest Bramah

87 GOD HATH MADE ME TO LAUGH
(*Gen. 21.6*)

When John the Bard said to the man who wrote these poems that he was one of the only two poets in Tyrone who had 'the right rhyme', he was admitting him to a fraternity as old as the heather-stills. It rhymes and it sings. You cannot follow the drums to *vers libre*, nor keep time to it with your fists on the table and your feet on the floor, nor dance to it in a loft. This poetry has memories of no paved streets or tiled houses unless when it boasts that

> When Derry was a village and Belfast a little town,
> We learned the holy Latin in Dungannon.

It goes to the tunes you pick up from a fiddler at fairs, or tagging with short legs behind the drums on the Twelfth, or from the likes of old Congo, about whom Mr Marshall has made a ballad: 'Most of his conversation was unprintable, but I never came in contact with a grander or more glorious imagination.' Full of big words he was, but he used them where they belonged. His stomach, he said himself, had a copper bottom; and the liquor he had put into it during his eighty years would float a battleship. 'His imagination wouldn't work until he had a good skinful, and that,' says his friend sadly, 'barred me from the best of him. It is only six weeks since he met me in Sixmilecross with the words: "A

141

vow to God a was jist goin' up to see ye in Castlerock. Tom Brown promised me a pair of trousers, an' Sammy Colhoun's givin' me a shirt, for when ye're goin' among dacent people ye hev to go dacent yerself."' He died in the workhouse hospital in January, very much as the Archpoet did in St Martin's cloister in Cologne. I think he 'went among dacent people', or, at any rate, as the Archpoet hoped, to 'the Country of the Laughing,' the men who like himself had the right rhyme.

Introduction to *Ballads and Verses from Tyrone* by W.F. Marshall

88 THINGS TOO HIGH
(*Ps. 131.1*)

FULBERT OF CHARTRES

The Abbot John, in stature small,
　　But not in godly graces,
Spake thus unto his elder friend
　– Both lived in desert places –

'I wish,' said he, 'to live secure
As angels do in heaven:
No food to eat, no garment wear
Whereon men's hands have striven.'

His senior said 'Be not too rash,
Brother, I counsel you,
For you may find you've bitten off
More than your teeth can chew.'

But he – 'Who goes not to the war
Nor falls, nor wins the fight.'
He spake, and to remoter wilds
Naked, went out of sight.

For seven days he painfully
Endured a grassy diet,
The eighth, his famine drove him home,
He can no more abye it.

Night, and the door fast shut, all snug
Sat in his cell the other,
When a faint voice without the door
Cries 'Open to me, brother.

'John, poor and needy, is without
The old familiar gate,
Let not your kindness scorn the man
Whom want did overtake.'

Then answered he, safe shut within:
'John to an angel turned him,
He contemplates the doors of heaven,
And men no more concern him.'

John had his bed without, and bore
The chills of night contrary,
And thus did penance rather more
Than was quite voluntary.

Now with the dawn, he's safe within,
And scorched with caustic sayings,
But he, intent upon his crust,
Endures it all with patience.

All warm again, he thanks returns
God and his friend unto,
And even tries, with feeble arm,
To wield the garden hoe.

Cured of his folly, he'll let him
An angel be who can,
Himself he finds it hard enough
To be a decent man.

More Latin Lyrics

89 RIDING UPON HIS ASS
(*Num. 22.22*)

The mediaeval church never much approved of wandering. One should not hasten to go from the place where one is to a place where one is not. Yet most of the great scholars were peripatetics sometime. Columbanus taught Greek metres from his eagle's perch at Bobbio, and St Peter himself met Coelchu on the road and carried his books for him. Gerbert's (Pope Sylvester II) early wanderings were a legend and a scandal. The Englishman, Adelard of Bath, came back from seven years' wandering in Asia Minor and Egypt and Arabia to write a book on natural history. When Buoncompagno fell out with the University of Bologna, he wrote a letter as from a scholar returned from conversation with Arabs and Satraps and the study of Uranath who maketh even the deaf asp to hear by his enchantments, and Catarath who distinguishes on the Astrolabe of Solomon, and Zinzaniath who interprets the barking of dogs, and then prepared, on a certain day in July, in the Piazza of St Ambrose, when the sun should be at its full heat, to turn an ass into a lion and thence into a winged fowl, in presence of the whole university. 'Yet in very truth in the end the ass shall remain.' On the appointed day the entire University, doctors and scholars, assembled in the Piazza and on the very roof tops and waited agape for the ass and the lion and the winged fowl. The heat was terrific, and at the end of several hours it dawned upon the University that the ass indeed remained.

'Scholares Vagantes'

90 ALL IS VANITY
(*Eccles. 1.2*)

'Marvel not', writes John of Salisbury to his friend Thomas Becket, 'that I climb no single step of that stair whereby alone men rise, for I despise those things which the courtiers go about, and the things I go about they despise. Marvel rather that I do not cut or break the knot, if there's no other way of loosing it, that so long has bound me to the trifles of the Court. Well nigh twelve years frittered away, I that had set my heart on things far other.' To both, disgrace brought deliverance. In 1159 John fell under the king's displeasure, was suspended, and left to struggle with his debts and the newly discovered *Organon* of Aristotle in a sudden delicious leisure. He used it to complete a defence of scholarship that swept it from the plane of intellectual delight to the eternity of the things of the spirit. But his hand, it seemed to him, had lost its cunning: gone 'the litheness of youth, the swiftness of ardent wits, the fidelity of memory'; and then, as always with him, the memory of Virgil comes to set upon his melancholy the consecration of an eternized phrase:

> 'The years take all away, aye, even the soul:
> A boy I can remember used to sing
> All the long summer days; now all the songs,
> The many songs he used to sing, forgotten.
> The voice has fled the singer: all is fled.

'The brevity of our life, the dullness of our senses, the torpor of our indifference, the futility of our occupation, suffer us to know but little; and that little is soon shaken and then torn from the mind by that traitor to learning, that hostile and faithless stepmother to memory, oblivion.'

'John of Salisbury'

145

91 EVERY MAN SHOULD EAT AND DRINK

(Eccles. 3.13)

John of Salisbury, driven out of England in the first gust of the king's anger, writes to his friend and master Thomas Becket, still beating against the wind. He is almost penniless; he had hardly twelve pence of his own when he left Canterbury, and the few marks given him were almost all spent in baggage and tips; lodgings in Paris are ruinous; he has had to sell his horses; he had thought to travel, but it looks more like sitting still. But the grumbling is transparent; the whole letter is radiant with escape. 'It seemed to me as soon as I touched these shores, that the very temper of the air was tenderer.' Paris, the second *patria* of scholars, is about him once again. 'Happy the exile to which such place is given!' So full in his heart, so apt the quotation, that he seems to have shared it with his old friend, Peter of Celle, now abbot of Rheims. The abbot kept open house for him:

> Happy exile indeed with rather more to drink than there is at home, and friends meeting one every day, and pleasant, fairly frequent little dinners. Ah, Paris! how apt art thou to capture souls! Exile? Would that my John did in very truth so think it, and would come back to his *patria*. Here is no buying of books, and paying of copyists, and wrangling of philosophers. Here is the school of the simplicity of Christ. Time was when you said you loved this place above all other places. You have greater friends now, but I loved you first.

John sends him his *Statesman's Book* for criticism; Peter retaliates with his own *De Panibus*, an allegorizing commentary of prostrating dullness on the various scriptural metaphors of bread. It was acknowledged with hearty affection, but with some levity:

> I swear it, I have swallowed every crumb of it, every crumb; but I need not remind a man of your experience that man doth not live by bread alone, and that an assiduity of potation hath made the English remarkable among foreign nations. Fitting is it that the hand which gave the bread should also pass the cup, and wine I know is readier to

your hand than *coelia* which the vulgar among us here call beer. Nevertheless I am myself a drinker of both, nor do I abhor anything that can make me drunk. Fail me and I brand you for a traitor, in that you have wedged me full of bread, and deny me the wine that might digest it, far unlike the custom of the French which is to send away the invited guest often, it is true, sober, but at least not dry.

'John of Salisbury'

You've two score, three score years before you yet,
And at the end of them your day is done.
A thousand plans you have before you set:
Is it worth while to weary over one?

Now, when the gods have made an idle day,
Take it, and let the idle hours go by;
And when the gods three cups before you lay,
Lift them, and drain them dry.

The world is weary, hasting on its road;
Is it worth while to add its cares to thine?
Seek for some grassy place to pour the wine,
And find an idle hour to sing an ode.

Lyrics from the Chinese

92 LET US NOT BE DESIROUS OF VAIN GLORY
(*Gal. 5.26*)

John was critical, certainly ironic, sometimes a little malicious, but he is never captious. There is nothing in him of the curious tendency which he notes as almost universal in humanity, to think ill of one's superiors in office. Read the comic poets, says John, or the tragic either, and will you ever find a *pater familias* popular with his household? It holds good of every profession, academic, religious, diplomatic. John's respect for Gilbert Foliot was profound; it always indeed went hard with him to quarrel with so elegant scholarship; but on Gilbert's one foible the hawk-like irony checks and stoops. In earlier days, Gilbert had had much to say to John about the morals of the religious orders; himself then entered the cloister, looked round upon his brethren and, kindled with new fires, inveighed upon the turpitude of his superiors. Gilbert is promoted: touched with sympathy for his fellow-officials, he yet feels that all is not well with Priors. They made Gilbert a prior: Gilbert now carps at Abbots. They made Gilbert an abbot: Gilbert's eye softens as it contemplates abbots, but bends itself sternly upon Bishops. They made Gilbert a bishop; and the Church hath rest.

'John of Salisbury'

TO A CENSORIOUS MONK   MARBOD OF RENNES

I give you no greeting, Geoffrey,
And I think you want none from me,
For you're in shaping to be an abbot,
And secure in your charity.
And as outlawed from God's kingdom
You shrink from the likes of me.

Yet the man who is sore burdened
With a bundle of sin on his back,
That man is loosed from the faggot
Should he turn from his wayward track:
The crown of clean life on his head
And the rewards of clean life in a stack,
For God's mercy is lavish and knows not
To measure itself by the peck.

More Latin Lyrics

93 SANCTIFIED THROUGH THE TRUTH
(*John 17.19*)

When John of Salisbury turns from Petronius Arbiter to the Book of Job – *Militia est, inquit, vita hominis super terram*: it does not matter that the language is the Latin of the *Polycraticus*: the accent is unmistakable, the accent one will hear again in Bacon and Burton and Sir Thomas Browne, in Addison and Swift: the detached and melancholy irony that is as English as *Havelok*.... In a note to Newman's *Apologia*, John of Salisbury appears among the English Saints, though in italics, 'as not included in the Sacred Catalogue'. John himself would have agreed, for his religion was of an admirable taciturnity; yet if his own definition of sainthood held, his place would be as eminent as Bernard's. In one of the most characteristic passages of his prose he borrows the fashion of the Stoics who are for ever busy with analogy, and after identifying the Greek *heron* with the Latin *verum*, that which is sure, he parallels it with the Catholic *sanctus*, that which is made fast, the souls who have escaped the perpetual flux of vanity and now inhabit truth. So too his valedictory request to the reader is not the familiar prayer for his soul's salvation, but that he may be 'truth's eager questioner, alike her lover and her worshipper'. It is this unemotional sincerity, this conviction that 'there is one sin, ignorance', that is John's strength, and if ever his style heightens to passion it is in defence of intellectual vision. The *Metalogicus*, the greatest defence of the scholar's religion that the Middle Ages produced, was goaded from him, rather in the spirit of those veterans and *emeriti* who came some years ago to Oxford to 'man the last ditch for Greek'.

'Is it not idle, this solicitude, this life of sleepless nights, laborious days, to win the secret places of philosophy?'

'John of Salisbury'

94 WE ARE ALSO HIS OFFSPRING
(*Acts 17.28*)

It was as well for the Church that John's hand was sometimes laid above the Archbishop's; it saved Henry himself from excommunication, and Christendom from yet another schism. John spent his strength and his lean purse and his hopes in fruitless negotiation. That moderating power, the clear-sighted detachment that would be inhuman but for its sensitiveness and its suffering, John had learned elsewhere. The scholar who had seen that in every darkness God hath his stars, that in every religion, Greek, Roman, Judaic, He is the shepherd of faithful souls, whose saints were pagan as well as Christian, Socrates, and Numa, and Scipio, and Titus, and above all his beloved Trajan, who cannot too much praise their fortitude, their chastity, their gentleness, could not be blind to Henry's angry virtues, his thwarted blundering zeal. John's soul was all its life a stranger, but he saw the earth with men upon it the stage of a comedy, but a pitiful one; for to most things, he says, there is a tragic end, and whether comedy or tragedy, it is to him 'immense, mysterious, unutterable'. He had known Becket arrogant, revengeful, unchristian; but he had also known Becket at the altar, celebrating in such wise that he saw the Lord's Passion. 'By doubting', Abelard had said, 'we are brought to question; and by questioning, we come at the truth.' That was John's way; but the other way of coming at the truth, Becket's way, the divine *furor*, he also recognized, and took the shoes from off his feet.

His own episcopate followed on the canonizing of the murdered Archbishop; but the familiar formula 'Dei gratia episcopus', altered in John's letters to 'John, by the Divine favour and the merits of St Thomas, servant of the Church at Chartres'. For it was at Chartres that John of Salisbury came in the phrase of his beloved Petronius, to the harbour of a stilled desire.

> Most happy I that unto my own lands
> Have leave to come at last. So fair a day!

> 'John of Salisbury'

95 SET YOUR AFFECTION
ON THINGS ABOVE
(*Col. 3.2*)

In these last decades of the century, the Cathedral stood a new and gracious miracle. Dead kings and queens, the familiar faces of Donatus and Plato and Aristotle looked down upon him, and through the blue of the western lancets he saw the light, as he had once seen it through a sapphire, 'become a purer heaven' – *firmamento puriori in sapphiro confirmatur* (Polycraticus v.3).

For four years he served the altar, the last of a long succession of saints and humanists. There are not many records of his episcopate, but two things are noted in the Necrology, that he secured the freedom of all serfs of the Cathedral, and forbade judgement by ordeal of water or fire. Peter of Celle bustles in for denial of accusations, John's quick temper, his slackness, his high-handedness, his indifference. John took little trouble to answer; he was safe in his old refuge.

Dear in many things, the dearest fruit of literature is this, that every grievous gulf of space and time annulled, it brings a man face to face with his friends. It hath a mysterious sweetness, this setting of the mind's edge to the reading or writing of something that hath worth. None of the things men do will they find so gracious as this, unless, moved by some divine compunction devotion urges to prayer or, the heart great with love, conceives the vision of God in the mind, and draws His greatness down as though with human hands.

It might well be that the Chapter had cause to grumble, and that the archdeacon found his bishop unbusinesslike. 'For we also wrestle with the Angel, and the man in whom the love of eternity hath kindled will go lame in the things of time. For not without the anguish of the struggle shall the face of truth be seen, nor shall the day break without a benediction.' It broke for John on the 25th of October 1180.

'John of Salisbury'

96 I WILL GO TO THE ALTAR OF GOD
(*Ps. 43.4*)

Chartres Cathedral was not built by princes or by public bodies; it was finished after a plague and a fire had impoverished and decimated the city and that gentle countryside; and free men and women carried stones from the quarry on their own backs, side by side with the straining oxen: and not only the stones, which one might feel had some promise of eternity about them, but fardels of meat and drink for the stomachs of the masons and the labourers at work there. The razed walls of Jerusalem where the foxes walked were reared again by each man building over against his own house: and it may be that the City of God will be built in no other way.

The Sunday Times, 10 June 1934

In the great age, the first half of the twelfth century, the stronghold of humanism is Chartres, Chartres where Donatus and Cicero and Aristotle still sit meditating on the west front of the cathedral. The rediscovery of the dignity of the human body which is in every sculpture of Chartres, of the beauty and abiding value of 'the whole sensible appearance of things' is brought to the twelfth century as to the sixteenth, by the Platonists. 'God creating the sun and moon' on the North portal of Chartres is the mediaeval and Puritan godhead, powerful and serene: but 'God creating the Day and the Night', that face of meditation and of dream, is the artist and the philosopher, as well as the moralist: the Logos in stone.

The Wandering Scholars

[Heloise] asked Gilles why Chartres had that strange compulsion, as though one's body worshipped, even before one's mind did: and he said that it had always been a sacred place, even among the Druids, that most of its bishops had been holy men, above all St Fulbert, who had built the Cathedral, and that the very streets were full of his presence still. Heloise had pondered: could the living and dying even of a holy man be remembered by arch and stone? Gilles had shrugged his shoulders. 'The habitation of God is with men,' he said briefly. 'And perhaps it is easier for a hard heart to quicken where one man has' — he hesitated — ' apprehended God.'

Peter Abelard

97 REMEMBER THE POOR
(*Gal. 2.10*)

With some of us the first reaction to this new scheme for the relief of unemployment was grim. No generation ever clears its mind of cant: it merely substitutes one species of it for another. But the cant most recently outmoded is the sentimental, the picturesque, the sham Gothic; and seen from that angle the Cathedral Pilgrimage becomes a kind of spiritual pub-crawl, a falsetto impertinence in the face of this Death-in-Idleness, the secret canker of the world.

Young men drifting like river weeds; decent middle-aged men warping and disintegrating like the timbers of a wharf that the sea has gone from for ever; a young mother crying in the police court because she has slipped out early and stolen a bottle of milk from the more prosperous doorstep round the corner, and been caught; a middle-aged woman with her head in a gas-oven because she cannot any longer endure the whingeing of small children never full fed.

And so one goes to visit the cathedral of one's choice on a bright July day, and the west door that is only opened for great Princes or the high feasts of the Church is opened for our pious pilgrimage, and we are aware of high emotion, a warming sense of unction and beneficence, for the price of the petrol or an excursion ticket, and the small additional sum of half a crown.

This is a genuine reaction: honest, as many follies are. But it is folly. No one pretends that all the half-crowns in England could cure what ails us; but they can at any rate make life more endurable for some of its victims; and it is worth lightening even by a fraction, the aggregate of human pain. It is true that every scheme for unemployment relief is a palliative and not a remedy; but there is something to be said for keeping the patient alive until the cure is found. And the cure will be found, when every individual conscience is uneasy enough to look for it. This business of the half-crowns is one way of reaching the individual conscience.

The Sunday Times, 10 June 1934

98 THE WORD WAS MADE FLESH
(*John 1.14*)

It is true that the scheme [for the relief of unemployment] is picturesque; that it is linked up with a journey to the oldest shrines in England, places, as Alcuin said of Lindisfarne, 'where men so valiant and saints so holy lie and take their rest'. Is it the worse for that? There is not so much old beauty left in the world that we can afford to gibe at the longing for it. It was this crazy temper, masking itself as reason, that turned the second greatest church in Christendom into a *haras*, a depot for stallions, and broke up, deliberately and piecemeal, nave and choir and apse of Cluny to supply an economical government with building material for its stables, till only the south transept,

> Even as an angel up at his great height
> Standing amid the light,

is left to take one's breath, as Ely does.

England has no great name in the arts, except in these two only, the art of the writing of poetry, the art of building in stone. With the first the least literate of us is familiar: but how many add to the names of Shakespeare and Milton and Keats and Blake and Donne the other harmony, of Canterbury and York and Durham and Wells and Norwich and Ely and, most remote and all but loveliest, St David's, hidden in a valley from the great Atlantic winds and its roofs crowned with the sea.

There was no risk of missing the way to Thomas Becket's house, said John of Salisbury: it was a beaten track, trodden by countless poor men's feet. That was written when Thomas was not yet Archbishop or martyr or saint, but plain Chancellor. Once again, after something like 800 years, there will be no risk of missing the way to Thomas Becket's house: from July 1 the West Door will be open for any man who comes to honour God and His saint in the person of His poor.

There is no creed to bar the pilgrimage. In these ancient houses no man but is welcome, even if to the faith that built them he has long been a stranger. It is enough that he has seen God hungry and fed Him. For there is one sentence in the Creed to which all men, Catholic and Communist, subscribe, whether they believe in Godhead or in manhood only; and with that high imagination which so often lies behind the rubric of tradition, it is the only sentence that brings a standing congregation to its knees: *Et incarnatus est.*

The Sunday Times, 10 June 1934

99 EVERY THING BY PRAYER
(*Phil. 4.6*)

Our heavenly Father, we have rejoiced this day in thy house, and we have felt the constraining of thy love. Thy blessing has come upon us; grant that it may be also upon those for whom we now pray.

Hear the prayers of brothers for sisters, of sisters for brothers, of parents for their children, and children for their parents, of friends for friends. We pray Thee for our absent loved ones. Keep them in life, keep them in growing honour.

We pray for the sick, for those over whom the rod of weariness hangs heavily. Be Thou their refuge and their strength, a very present help in this, their time of trouble. Bring them back to health and strength, if it be thy will. Be present with the dying. Come to them, as their everlasting Father, receive them in thine arms, soothe them as a mother doth her child; may they depart fearing no evil and so be for ever with Thee.

And our God, we remember those who are in mourning this day for some loved one, those whose wounds the angel of Death has opened afresh. Be with them in their distress: fill their hearts with thy love. May their sorrow be as a cloud over the sun, enabling them to gaze into the heavens lit with thy glory.

Be with thy servants in every land who seek to bring to men the glad tidings of thy Gospel of peace. May the day in which men strive against men be ended, that the day when swords shall be turned into ploughshares may come upon the earth.

155

Be with thy Church everywhere. May she walk warily in times of peace and quietness, and boldly in times of trouble. Do Thou remove all harshness and bitterness from amongst us, towards those who walk not in all things with us, but who worship our Lord in sincerity and truth.

And all this we ask for the sake of thy dear Son.

Unpublished notebook (undated)

Part Seven

AS THE DEW
OF HERMON

'Behold, how good and pleasant it is
for brethren to dwell together in unity!
.... As the dew of Hermon, and as
the dew that descended upon the
mountains of Zion: for there the Lord
commanded the blessing, even life
for evermore.'

Ps. 133. 1–3

100 HEAR MY CRY, O GOD
(*Ps. 61.1*)

Lord, we thy servants come, seeking and praying Thee to accept us. Let our sins be hidden from Thee, let not our iniquities and our transgressions come before Thee, but do Thou hear, forgive, and save. Thine ear is not heavy that it cannot hear, nor thine arm short that it cannot save. Save us now; forgive our many wrongdoings; give us grace to confess them in a true spirit. Turn to us again, O God of our salvation. We have sinned, we have wronged Thee, our Father, we have turned away from Thee, thinking we know better, as children will, but we have found out that thy way is the only way. In thy mercy hear, forgive, and save.

Make us new, ready and willing to be Christian in everything. Make us charitable, long-suffering, and full of mercy to those who have done us ill, even as Thou has shown Thyself merciful to us who have wronged Thee. Make us gentle in thought and word, and in our action to our fellows; enable us to bear in mind thy love to us, that we may love our enemies, do good to those who hate us and use us despitefully. Make us patient, ready to bless, slow to anger. Enable us to go cheerfully about our occupations, that the ready hand and pleasant smile of a good and humble spirit may dwell with us. Be Thou our guide and our counsellor. May we look to Thee not only in troublous times when Death walks abroad and fear and trembling go hand-in-hand, but may we live in Thee and with Thee, when the voice of joy and safety fills our heart.

These our humble desires we ask Thee to grant, knowing that when Thou dost give Thou givest above all we ask or think. So do to us this day. We ask it in Christ's name, and to Thee, God almighty, Father, Son and Holy Spirit, shall be the praise.

Unpublished notebook (undated)

101 THE DOGS EAT OF THE CRUMBS
(*Matt. 15.27*)

He was a shabby little dog, and he was thin. He was sitting on the doorstep when I came down one morning, very early, before anyone was up. I think he had been there all night. But he jumped up when the door opened, and trotted a little way down the path, and then he stopped and turned round and looked at me with big frightened eyes, and began wagging his tail. He had such imploring eyes that it hurt to look at them; and when I got down on my knees beside him and patted his untidy little head he gave a little choked bark that was half a whine, and the tail wagged so hard that all the small body seemed wagging too. But he still looked at me, and his eyes were very hungry. So I said, 'Wait, Doggie, until I get you something to eat'.... Coming back I thought I heard a yelp, and when I got to the door the milk boy was standing there grinning, and away, away down the road I saw a little dog running as hard as it could go. The milk boy said he was a dirty wee beast, and he had just kicked him out of that.

That was years ago, and every now and then I remember him, and it hurts even yet, and then I began thinking how queer it was that one should care so much, just in a minute, for a little strange dog; and from that I began thinking that if we could really feel that God cares as much about us, if it were only for five minutes out of our whole lives, as I had cared about a little dog, it would make all the difference.

There are so many people for Him to think about, He can't possibly care, really care about each one of us? But there is one word in the Catechism – God is 'infinite'. It is a hard word but what it means is that God is so big that there is enough of Him for everybody. So instead of thinking of the crowds and crowds of people He has to care about, just think how very, very big his heart must be. I nearly broke my heart for a little dog, so think how much tenderness there must be in God. God is so much bigger that He can care for far more people, and so much kinder that He can care much harder. He is like the sea: you can fill buckets and buckets, and there is just as much left as when you began. Only He is bigger and kinder than the sea.

So the next time you are afraid about anything, and the next time you think you are so horrid nobody could like you much, and the next time

160

you feel lonely and out of things, remember that God cares, cares what becomes of you, and cares terribly — far, far more than you would care for a little hungry dog.

Stories from Holy Writ (Foreword)

102 THEY BROUGHT UNTO HIM ALSO INFANTS
(*Luke 18.15*)

This time it is a harder thing, that we will never quite understand. Why does God let people be hurt if He really cares? Why did He let that little dog I told you about go hungry? And not only him but all the children who haven't enough to eat, and all the people who are crying and are sick and sad. Now nobody but God himself will ever quite answer it. I'm going to tell you a story not about a dog but about a boy, little and hungry and poor, and a doctor, who wasn't very rich but was always looking out for little children who had nowhere to go and bringing them home, until at last his house was full. So when a little boy came up to him one night in the street and begged to be taken home, the doctor didn't know what to do; he thought of the crowd at home and how hard it was to get them enough to eat. So he shook his head and said he would try in a day or two. But somehow he couldn't get the boy out of his head, and went out to look for him all the next day, and took a lantern and went out again at night. This time he found him. He was lying curled up in an old barrel, and the doctor ran to waken him and tell him he had come to take him home. And then he saw that he was too late. The boy was dead.

It broke his heart. Standing there in the rain beside the old barrel, the doctor promised God that he would never turn any child away again. He gave his whole life to it, got other people to help him, and saved thousands and thousands of little children. And all because of one little lad. God had to let him die, because He knew it would break the doctor's heart. Maybe some who read this will remember a verse that says, 'It is expedient that one man should die.'

There are two things I want you to remember. You can't help the great

161

big pain of the world, but you can be kind your own self, and never hurt anyone if you can help it, and Christ will keep you tender of heart. And if ever you think God is hard and cruel, remember that whatever hurts us is hurting Him too. 'In all their afflictions, He was afflicted.' And remember that to make us sure of it, He came down Himself out of heaven and lived along with us, and suffered in the end far more terribly than He will ever let any one of us.

Daybreak, August 1914

103 GIVE ME UNDERSTANDING
(*Ps. 119.73*)

It's about ten, and I'm back from church and just had supper. I'm glad I went to Dr Hutton tonight. It was on 'We know not whither Thou goest ... I am the Way.' He began about Christ's promise of a spiritual presence – How much of our thinking is *really* about material things? Man after man in the street, but the mind behind the face is working over again that quarrel with a friend yesterday, that broken hope, that undeserved failure. Speak to him and he'll answer with cheerfulness and gusto – the heroic human convention that hides a troubled spirit. But we live with ghosts.

Christ never answered a question. He knew no answer is of any use to us except what we find for ourselves. But I once worked under a great mathematical genius. He never lectured but we could bring him any problem we had, and he would put down his pen and look at us. 'Sir, I can't see how ...' 'But don't you see?' And nine times out of ten, we saw. There was something about that naked intellect that quickened one's own beyond recognition. That is Christ's way. 'Jesus steadfastly set his face to go to Jerusalem and after that ...' I have my moods, all of us have them, when I ask uncomfortable questions about life, especially my own life, and am grieved and indignant at my unmerited misfortunes. It cures me if I have to go and see someone in St Thomas's or Bart's. It's true. All the way to church, I'd been fighting down dull despondence – I'd go on in the wilderness till I was too old to be anything but a hack, all because of eight wasted years of doing my duty as I saw it. But tonight has shut me up, I hope for life. Never ask questions about Absolutes. The absolute becomes relative when it touches you. It has linked up in my head with that picture in Ben Hur, the cross swaying and stumbling above the heads of the crowd. That shuts your mouth.

To Meg (undated)

104 A PATTERN TO THEM HEREAFTER
(*1 Tim. 1.16*)

PETRONIUS ARBITER

Nealce, be that night for ever dear,
The night that laid you first upon my heart.
Dear be the couch, the quiet burning lamp,
And you, so tender, come into my power.
Still let us love, although the years be hasting,
And use the hours that brief delay is wasting.
Old love should last: O Love, do thou forfend
That what was swift begun, were swift to end.

TO HIS WIFE   AUSONIUS

Love, let us live as we have lived, nor lose
The little names that were the first night's grace,
And never come the day that sees us old,
I still your lad, and you my little lass.
Let me be older than old Nestor's years,
And you the Sibyl, if we heed it not.
What should we know, we two, of ripe old age?
We'll have its richness, and the years forgot.

Mediaeval Latin Lyrics

105 LET US NOT JUDGE ONE ANOTHER
(*Rom. 14.13*)

I wish sometimes you would cut the moral 'austere man' aspect of God out of your mind, and accustom yourself to a more wayside God, a Man that other men wanted to go along with, before they thought of their sins or repentance. Did you ever think – it has just come to me now – that St John never said, 'He that is chaste dwelleth in God, and God in him'? It was, 'He that loveth dwelleth in God.'

You know, the one thing I learned out of those last years in Cedar Avenue, was that to hate is to be in hell. I didn't actually hate Mother: but I had a deep festering grudge aginst all the ways she had thwarted me, the things she had taken from me, and never a word of thanks. All the sacrifices were on her side. After she was dead, I suddenly saw my own heart. And I knew that if only I had mastered that grudge inwardly as well as outwardly, those years would have been far richer. I suppose death helps to put things under the countenance of eternity. It wasn't that I was sorrier for her after she died – it was partly my pity for her that used to drive me so crazy: a mixture of anger and pity comes near murder. It was that I had let a grievance poison myself, and a grievance is a kind of cancer of the heart.

I have so marvelled at you all these years, not only your courage, but your soundness and sweetness. Don't let the dark tide that is in us all, of littleness against man and God, come any higher. Generosity is far more important than any chastity, and don't constrict God's infinity of kindness by making bargains with Him. 'No man can redeem his brother' – it sounds menacing, but not when the reason for it comes – 'for the redemption of the soul is precious'.

To Meg, 9 August 1935

Truth of all truth,
O Life, O Truth, O Way,
Who by the strait paths of Thy Truth
Drivest our sin beyond the threshold of our door,
To thee, Incarnate Word,

Faith, Hope, and Charity
Continually do cry.

Thou Who dost set Thy prisoner at Thy bar, and then
Makest him a man again,
And for that forespent carnal ecstasy,
Givest such grace,
That he accounts him blessed.
O miracle of strength!
O kingly word,
That once a sick man heard,
'Arise, take up thy bed, and go thy way.'

More Latin Lyrics

106 THE GREATEST IS CHARITY
(*1 Cor. 13.13*)

I thought of poor Beatrice [Blackett] alone in that Chinese puzzle of a flat, and reproached myself for ever grousing about her passion for companionship. And in short, for ever grousing about anything.

Because if one loves, one really isn't lonely: it is the unloving heart that is always cold, and has no fire to warm itself at. 'Beloved, let us love one another, for love is of God; and he that loveth is born of God, *and knoweth God.*' Don't tell me there are theological explanations of it – that the love must be 'in Christ'. He that loveth, knoweth God. Which means that it is when one's heart goes out to anything, it is, in that moment, close to God. And what if it were really true, that the power at the back of all this cruel universe were love? Love as we know it. It's no wonder Dante said when he saw that vision of 'love that moves the sun and the stars', that it was *tanto olraggio* – a kind of outrage on his being. For to come within the least whisper of it is to leave one gasping.

I begin to see what happened to Abelard, when he saw that the Holy Ghost was love, and that the whole world lay in it, moved by it, the love of God the Father and God the Son.

One writes it, and it is trite – the familiar commonplace that we've

165

heard from our cradles. But if ever one comes within its breath, it is so terrible that one almost looks about for familiar little shelters of noises and buses to shut out the stars. 'There shall no man see Me and live.'

And so the Son of Man comes eating and drinking, it being the only way in which human beings can endure to apprehend God.

To Meg, 1935

Earth's self shall go and the swift wheel of heaven
Perish and pass, before our love shall cease.
Do but remember me, as I do thee,
And God, who brought us on this earth together,
Bring us together in his house of heaven.

Mediaeval Latin Lyrics

107 FATHER, FORGIVE
(*Luke 23.34*)

Your tiny letter has done me more good than anything. The truth is, I think, I'm suffering from shell-shock. You and I are dreadfully sensitive to violence; it does something very queer to our minds. The wire first and then the letter were like the scream of a shell. I just lay down to get my heart steady, and then brewed myself a very strong cup of tea.

I suppose it was madness but last night, sitting here writing and listening to the Good Friday music from Parsifal, I suddenly saw the love of God that does not even wait for us to be sorry – that tried to *make* us sorry, by its own absolute sacrifice and agony. The violins went on and on, and I suddenly saw. I saw us all comfortable at our firesides, and all respectable; and outside that lone wolf, with its health and reputation gone, and the pain in its eye, and me ready to stone it from the door. And I just wrote it the most loving letter I've ever written, telling how I'd seen a wolf that night that wasn't a wolf at all, but only ill and frightened and mad, and to come back to 'that great Shepherd of the sheep', and live the days that were left in peace and honour, and I would try to send 15/- a week. And for fear I should know it was madness in the morning, I went out and posted it.

What do you think? The thing that has always broken me is the generosity of that 'Neither do I condemn thee; go and sin no more.' And it came on me last night that if I stopped stoning and just wiped it all out, it might cast out the devil. Anyhow I learned things last night about Good Friday. I had a feeling that I must stay here alone this Easter – I mean, I had to, about that lecture: but all the same, I could have filled up the evenings with people and theatres. But I felt I mustn't. And sure enough. It was the kind of thing I've written in *Abelard*, and it came on again. I have felt the *absoluteness* of God before – 'the Light that no man can approach unto' – but never His compassion. So whether it's worth it to another or not, it was worth it to me.

To Meg (undated)

108 DO JUSTLY AND LOVE MERCY
(*Mic. 6.8*)

Sir, – I write as an Ulsterwoman, jealous for the good name of my province. Six boys, the eldest of them 21, have been found guilty of shooting for political reasons at a patrol car in Belfast and murdering a policeman. They are to be hanged, collectively, on 2 September. The Attorney-General of Northern Ireland has refused to allow the case to be tried before the supreme tribunal of English justice, the justice to which Northern Ireland has always appealed. Is his case then so weak that it is unable to support the journey to Westminster? And is the memory of a kindly Ulster policeman to become a thing of horror in men's minds, like the memory of Heydrich, thanks to the savagery of his avengers?

Yours, etc.

HELEN WADDELL

To the Editor of *The Times*, 27 August 1942

. . . The day is nigh at hand
The day of wrath and vengeance,
And darkness on the land.

Day of thick clouds and voices,
Of mighty thundering,
A day of narrow anguish
And bitter sorrowing.

Mediaeval Latin Lyrics

109 A WORKMAN THAT NEEDETH NOT TO BE ASHAMED

(2 Tim. 2.15)

I began to read the proofs of a book by a headmaster on education with the sirens for Alert and All-Clear succeeding one another like the arms of a windmill in perpetual lamentation, and the odd little beasts that are the latest invention of the most highly-educated nation in Europe roaring and ranting through a cloudless heaven, then falling silent like a hawk poised over its quarry, before the crash and the scream of the kill. But the spirit of the book that I was reading defied them: reasonable, passionate, humane. I could not lay it down till I had finished it, and I finished it in an exaltation, the exaltation of Bernard Shaw's greatest, and unrecorded, phrase. It was an argument at lunch on the value of vivisection in medical research. 'The thing is cruel,' said the famous biologist who was defending it, 'but it is a cruel necessity.' 'If it is cruel', said G.B.S., 'it is not a necessity. If a thing is cruel it is wrong, and if a thing is wrong it is not necessary, it is not even *expedient*. Let men once make up their minds to that, and shut the door – and they will find another. For there is nothing beyond the power of the spirit of man.'

The silence that fell on us when G.B.S. finished speaking came upon me again as I read the last paragraphs of this schoolmaster's plea for the children, for something more than utility in education. 'Education is spiritual in essence and therefore it is the spirit of the thing that counts. You may house your boys and girls in palaces, but this will make little difference unless they are taught by princes.' . . . . Once, he went on, prehistoric man trained his sons to the making of weapons that they might survive in the struggle for existence. Then, even in religion, even in science, came the struggle for power. 'If we adopt the utilitarian

168

outlook on education, our aim differs little from that of our ancestors, except that we endeavour to clothe our sons and daughters with an armour of banknotes instead of one of mail. . . . If education is to mean anything at all, the breath of God must sweep through it from the turrets and spires of Oxford to the humblest country elementary school. . . . Children, parents, teachers, Ministers of Education, let us desire, imagine, will and create. . . . Let us dream the type . . . that we wish to create.'

The crazy diabolic symphony of power was still vibrant overhead, strange counterpoint to the cry of this passionate dreamer. Then, accepting, transfiguring, harmonising both, the echo of a still mightier singing –

> to hope till Hope creates
> From its own wreck the thing it contemplates.

Article in *On Education* by W.H. Crowe, London 1944

110 HE THAT ENDURETH TO THE END SHALL BE SAVED
(*Matt. 10.22*)

We went to Canterbury yesterday where instead of evensong, we found a special service for Youth Fellowship. Young men came up the aisle with their little tin banners for each country – at least half of them dark-skinned – and laid them against the entrance to the choir: and on one of them I saw 'Tokio', and my heart turned over.

I was absorbed in the sermon by the Bishop of Croydon, a young man; and at the end of the 'book of words' for that particular service, there was this sentence which I didn't recognize as one of the collects: 'O Lord God, when Thou givest to thy servants to endeavour any great matter, grant us also to know that *it is not the beginning, but the continuing of the same unto the end, until it be thoroughly finished,* which yieldeth the true glory: through Him who for the finishing of Thy work laid down his life, our Redeemer Jesus Christ, Amen.' It suddenly came on me that my despairing thoughts about my own small piece of work, the feeling that it makes no difference whether I do it or not – what's the use? – that *there* is the canker in my life and that not to finish the work I have begun is a sin – what the Desert Fathers called *accidia,* a kind of melancholy that paralyses the soul. 'Whatsoever thy hand findeth to do, do it with all thy might.' It is partly humility, partly fatigue, but already I have begun to feel a kind of rustling among the leaves.

To Meg, 1944

Part Eight

COME,
LORD JESUS

'And the Spirit and the
bride say, Come. And let him that
heareth say, Come. And let him
that is athirst come. And whoever will,
let him take the water of Life freely....
Amen. Even so, come, Lord Jesus.'

Rev. 22.17, 20

111 PRAISE YE HIM, ALL HIS ANGELS
(*Ps. 148.2*)

MS. tenth century

Angelic host,
Phalanx and squadron of the Prince-Archangels,
Uranian power,
Strength of the gracious word,

Spirits that have dominion, Cherubim,
Divine tribunal of the air,
And Seraphim with flaming hair,

And you, O Michael, Prince of heaven,
And Gabriel, by whom the word was given,

And Raphael, born in the house of Life,
Bring us among the folk of Paradise.

Mediaeval Latin Lyrics

112 THE SABBATH OF REST
(*Exod. 31.15*)

White clouds are in the sky.
Great shoulders of the hills
Betwen us two must lie.
The road is rough and far
Deep fords between us are.
I pray you not to die.

Lyrics from the Chinese

LAMENT FOR HATHIMODA,
ABBESS OF GANDESHEIM

Thou hast come safe to port,
    I still at sea.
The light is on thy head,
    Darkness in me.
Pluck thou in Heaven's field
    Violet and rose
While I strew flowers that will thy vigil keep
Where thou dost sleep
Love in thy last repose.

More Latin Lyrics

113 WRITTEN IN HEAVEN
(*Luke 10.20*)

'*The wind bloweth where it listeth, and thou hearest the sound thereof, but canst not tell whence it cometh nor whither it goeth..*' It is the accepted metaphor, in a book of great metaphor for the way of the Holy Ghost. Yet Christ applied it differently. 'So,' He said, '*is every man that is born of the Spirit.*' It is as though something of the mystery, some depth of the eternity from which their life drew, 'an ampler ether, a diviner air', should be about those born, not of the will of the flesh, nor of the will of man, but of God. Abraham the Hebrew, the Man from beyond the River, had it, above all the saints of the older faith; St John, above all the disciples of our Lord: St Francis of Assisi, beyond all men since. It is an untranslatable grace; it leaves small record. Simply one knows that there are pages in St John's Gospel where the air is never still; fragments of our Lord's discourses flung like boulders where the great winds have passed: stray sentences in unexpected places that bring with them

Murmurs and scents of the infinite sea

and lives of one's own knowing to which men brought their sick – tarnished hope and impotent desire – that at the least the shadow passing by might fall on them and they be healed.

174

'What went ye into the wilderness to see?' asked our Lord concerning John the Baptist. 'A reed shaken with the wind?' In another sense than His, it was what one did see in Dr Isabel Mitchell. One had always that curious double sense of the fragility of the body, and the resistless strength of the spirit that swayed it. Even in childhood some remarked on the clear pallor and the 'bright and shining grey eyes' – eyes that might have been the very colour of the wind – and prophesied that she would never grow up. Some who saw her for the first time on her last furlough – she was seriously ill just then, and the burden of the 'closed gate' at Fakumen was very heavy upon her – have carried ever since the memory of a white face almost transparent in the fire that consumed her, and the spirit like a flame in her eyes. It was not that she was sickly: she went scatheless through childhood, a little less robust than the others, but charmed, for all her fragile looks, against infection. Until the medical examination that passed her for foreign service she had never, she used to boast, 'shown her tongue to a doctor.' It was simply that the spirit of life, the 'electric spark in the alabaster vase,' showed more plainly in her than in others: looking at her, it was easy to accept Milton's thought of the soul, as not so much indwelling as transfused.

She was born in Belfast in 1879: the daughter of a busy Manse and a busy parish, for Belfast has few more faithful ministers than the Rev. D.K. Mitchell of Crumlin Road Presbyterian Church.

Yet Isabel's vocation needs something to account for it beyond temperament and heredity and training. Some, not the least faithful, have gone to work such as hers rather from the intangible, unresting pressure of home influence and expectation than from an inward compulsion, and in the fields white unto harvest, to their great gain. Some, again, have gone, not grudgingly, but from the slow dogged conviction that this was the will of God concerning them. But to a few, there was no other way possible. Their eyes have seen the King, the Lord of Hosts. 'So the vision reveals the debt, to the humblest as well as to the highest.' '*Thine eyes shall see the King in His beauty: they shall behold the land that is very far off.*' How could it be otherwise? Can we limit the grace of such a King? Francis of Assisi, kneeling before the crucifix, saw the Crucified, and at the same time heard the weary call of many lands. Carey saw Him – and India: Morrison saw Him – and China: Livingstone saw Him – and Africa. 'Twice,' wrote one who was with her in Manchester the winter before her designation, 'I saw her face lit with radiance that was nothing but divine: once at her last service in Grosvenor Square. It happened to be Communion, and we were singing

Were the whole realm of nature mine,
That were an offering far too small;
Love so amazing, so divine,
Demands my soul, my life, my all.

She was standing where I could see her face, and it was transfigured.'

It is a great saying of Dr Alexander Maclaren that the glory of the Transfiguration was not fully revealed till Christ came down from the mountain with no shining on His face, and freed a devil-ridden boy from the demon that possessed him. More than any other perhaps, that experience and that disillusioning and that hope is for the medical missionary. Day by day his Lord and he come together in the sacrament of the broken bodies of men, together taking upon them their infirmities and bearing their sickness. Those who knew her afterwards, who knew how all but visibly it was 'the Healer of Gennesaret' who walked her rounds with her, could hardly imagine her otherwise. Yet it was not of her own choosing. She is not the only missionary to whom that has happened; who has had to suffer the ingrafting of an alien interest, 'for the riches of the world' and of themselves. One does not often remember the passion with which the Apostle of the Gentiles entreated that he might glorify his Lord among his own people. 'I said, Lord, they know that I imprisoned and beat in every synagogue them that believed on Thee: and when the blood of Thy martyr Stephen was shed, I also was standing by and consenting unto his death. And He said unto me, "Depart; for I will send thee far hence unto the Gentiles."' With her it was something more than an ingrafting: it was also, in St Paul's phrase, a 'diminishing'. She had a great love for literature; the creative restiveness was in her; and all her life she was wistful after the lost discipline of a critical training in Arts. It was not easy at eighteen to give up the work that seemed already her inheritance; and at Queen Margaret Hall she eyed the Arts students with great wistfulness. It seemed a small thing: academic training can be as barren as academic distinction; but those who know the potential richness of it, its brief perfect satisfaction, will not lightly misinterpret 'the accent of that closing door.' It was in 1897 that her choice was made. Very early she had heard the 'cry from pitiable places'; the burden of the women had always been with her.

But there was another element in her preparation. 'Also the word of the Lord came unto me saying, Son of Man, behold I take away from thee the desire of thine eyes with a stroke; yet neither shalt thou mourn nor weep. So I spoke unto the people in the morning and at even my wife died: and I did in the morning as I was commanded.'

They were the two youngest, Isabel, and the brother born on her fifth birthday. There is motherhood in that relationship always, even where the brother is older: the woman who has cared for a brother is not childless. He taught her that: and then taught her the sharpness of death. The two were inseparable 'minding the same things'. He, as well as she, was determined to be a medical missionary: she coached him in the vacations, in the intimacy of work that is even a better thing than the intimacy of play. In the summer of 1902 they had planned to work together at the sea: she was to coach him for a second year's scholarship at Queen's; the boy was eighteen then. He had gone with his father for a cycling tour in the County Derry hills, and the two were expected home on 3 September. The evening before, his sister had gone out to the rocks to watch the sunset, and stayed there a long while alone. The glory of it broke that night in a storm of wind and rain. Word came the next day that the boy had spent the night in a country manse, and had gone out in the early morning to bathe, when the river came down in spate. They found his body three days later.

'Perhaps he therefore departed for a season, that thou shoulds't receive him for ever'. So our Lord went away, that his disciples might look for Him in the faces of the least of his brethren. So Herod stretched out his hand and slew James the brother of John with the sword, that the Church might find its greatest lover, and all men a brother in him. Even so Isabel received her brother: in the faces of little Chinese children; in her tenderness for all young things in a world that had suddenly grown old, so that the glimpse of a boy's face passing in the twilight could wring her heart into a passion of prayer for his unknown youth; in her acquaintance with grief, through that one breach that let in the sea –

> Desperate tides of the whole great world's anguish,
> Forced through the channels of a single heart,

in the gaiety that had known pain in its ecstasy, and now need fear nothing any more, in the mystery of the Perpetual Presence.

St James, no less than St Peter and St John, shared in the closer intimacy, the deeper initiation, of the Three Companions, yet he died after short service, and left no memorial. Only that a great while after, a book was written surer of eternity than time and in it 'the great vision of the guarded mount' of the young men who follow the Lamb whithersoever He goeth. *These were redeemed from among men the first fruits unto God and to the Lamb. And in their mouth was found no guile, for they are without fault before the throne of God.* After that, an Epistle, wherein an old man argued from the love of the brother whom he had seen to the Love of the unseen God. Last of all, a Gospel, where the solitude of a lifetime flowered in the Secret Rose of the Mystics, the doctrine of the indwelling Christ.

In Manchuria they called her their St John.

Tribute to Dr Isabel Mitchell (unpublished)

HIBERNICUS EXUL

The dead limbs lie, as Adam first begat them,
O Christ, O Life, come down
The dead limbs lie.

Thou shalt raise up the dead from the dust of the earth,
When the clear trumpet sounds.
Thou shalt raise up the dead.

Gather these ashes in, for store in heaven,
O hands that made them,
Gather these ashes in.

More Latin Lyrics

114 BRING MY SOUL OUT OF PRISON
(*Ps. 142.7*)

PRUDENTIUS

Take him, earth, for cherishing,
To thy tender breast receive him.
Body of a man I bring thee,
Noble even in its ruin.

Once was this a spirit's dwelling,
By the breath of God created.
High the heart that here was
beating,
Christ the prince of all its living.

178

Guard him well, the dead I give thee,
Not unmindful of His creature
Shall He ask it: He who made it
Symbol of His mystery.

Comes the hour God hath appointed
To fulfil the hope of men,
Then must thou, in very fashion,
What I give, return again.

Not though ancient time decaying
Wear away these bones to sand,
Ashes that a man might measure
In the hollow of his hand:

Not though wandering winds and idle,
Drifting through the empty sky,
Scatter dust was nerve and sinew,
Is it given man to die.

Once again the shining road
Leads to ample Paradise;
Open are the woods again
That the Serpent lost for men.

Take, O take him, mighty Leader,
Take again thy servant's soul,
To the house from which he
wandered
Exiled, erring, long ago.

But for us, heap earth about him,
Earth with leaves and violets strewn,
Grave his name, and pour the fragrant
Balm upon the icy stone.

Mediaeval Latin Lyrics

115 I AM THE RESURRECTION AND THE LIFE
(*John 11.25*)

ON THE DEATH OF HER BROTHER GEORGE, 15 JUNE 1915

My Father,
I can only write to you a very little. Dear, do not break your heart for me, but I had bad news this morning. It is my brother, the one just older than I am, the George that you said was called for you. He died very suddenly last night of heart failure. He had gone to the South on Monday to stay for a little with Eileen's people — he was engaged to her. He was so dear that I think Christ looking upon him loved him. And we cared for each other so much that nothing can take him from me. . . . My father, it was a perfect death — to go straight into God's love from the dearest love he knew.

> The good, the better, and the last the best,
> This is the order of the master's wine.

[Her letter of the following week completed the natural sequence of events:]

My Father,
. . . They sang the twenty-third psalm at his burying — a great company of them; the men who liked him so, and sang it to 'Martyrdom'. I chose it instead of the Burial Psalms, because it is a psalm of the living, and not of the dead. And when they came to

> And in God's house forever more
> My dwelling-place shall be,

the peace of God came down upon the house. And I was satisfied at last. It seemed to take away something that was crushing my heart.

The evening that they brought him home was the hardest. I know now what made Abraham pray that he might bury his dead out of sight. The coffin lay there on the velvet pall with the flowers heaped round it, and I knew that George was inside it, dead. I did not feel him near me any more. I could not even remember him. And I lay that night and thought of him, but it was George dead that I thought of, lying under the flowers.

And then – I think one writes some chapters of the Bible in blood – I seemed to be living the eleventh chapter of John. Jesus said to her, 'Thy brother shall rise again,' and Martha answered – I know how drearily – 'I know that he shall rise again at the resurrection at the last day.' Jesus saith unto her, 'I am the Resurrection and the Life. He that believeth in Me though he were dead, yet shall he live, and whosoever liveth and believeth in Me shall never die.'

> 'Believeth thou this?'
> Martha said unto him, 'Yea, Lord.'

And so I fell asleep.

The sun shone on him for his burying, just as it had shone for his ordaining. All his brothers had come to him; the four men that he cared for most, all ordained within a few months of him, came that morning and stood around him in a sore dumb agony; they took the last lift. And Meg and I watched him go out into the sunlight; it was as if he went out on a great wave of love. He loved more than any man I ever knew, and it was given him – pressed down and running over.

Donoughmore sent him a great anchor, white lilies and purple violets, with this simply written 'From his sorrowing congregation'. Meg and I brought him a cross of white iris, with blue iris at its heart. And we hid our card in it, because the message was for his own self. 'I thank my God for every remembrance of you.' I think I shall have it on his burial stone.

He was no saint, my father, he was terribly human. But in one thing at least he was Christ's man, and that was his heart. He's in every verse of that thirteenth chapter of Corinthians.

My father, I must say good-night. Don't be grieving that wonderful heart of yours for me. For I am utterly content. And if I miss him – well, there's a line in Terence that haunted me long after I read it – 'In truth, he hath deserved to be remembered of you.'

Ever since last Wednesday the sun has shone, and the world has been in 'an air of glory'. And on Sunday, though it was a strange church, the text was 'the power of an endless life', and the hymns, 'My God, I thank Thee' and 'O Love that will not let me go.'

> My heart restores its borrowed ray,
> That in Thy sunshine's blaze its day
> May brighter, fairer be.

'His sunshine's blaze', that's where the boy is now. I can't write to you about your last letter. Your love comes round me like a shield.

To Dr Taylor, 23 June 1915

Postscript a week later:

My Father, I am not unhappy. I think the Valley of the Shadow is a little like the Valley of Humiliation, where Heartsease grew. On the Sunday after he died, I went out into a sunny green field with my nephew Charles, and saw the first wild roses. It was the sharpest thing that ever happened to me. These things belonged to him somehow. It would have seemed easier if he had died in winter. And days after, someone in the train had a great basket of red roses, and it wakened again. You will understand now what went to the writing of this:

> It had been easy to wind you
>   Your winding sheet of the snows.
> What have I done that I find you
>   Dead in the heart of a rose?

I have just seen a little snap of Geo, taken at the door of his Manse. It was one of the boys who was down seeing him, and snapped him the June morning before he went South. It's the great old house thick with ivy, such a promise of peaceful habitation in it, only that the windows are blank and empty. And the boy who was never to live in it is in the doorway, too small for me to see his face, but just the easy way he used to stand, with his great height and the long legs. And there is such a promise of summer about him, the grass on either side of the path high to the knee, and in it masses of poppies and tall white daisies. It was so like his life – on the doorstep of a house untenanted.

And it's good to remember looking at it, 'In my Father's house are many mansions.'

To Dr Taylor, 30 June 1915

ALCUIN

> Come, make an end of singing and of grieving,
> But not an end of love.
> I wrote this song, beloved, bitter weeping,
> And yet I know 'twill prove

That by God's grace,
We two shall see each other face to face,
And stand together with a heart at rest.

More Latin Lyrics

116 UNTIL THE DAY DAWN
(*2 Pet. 1.19*)

ALCUIN

Brief is our life, now in the midst of the years,
And death with silent footfall draweth near.
His dreaded fingers are upon the gates,
And entering in, takes all thou hast.
Look forward to that day, and to that unloved hour
That when Christ come from heaven
He find the father of the house still watching,
And then thou shalt be blessed.
Happy the day when thou shalt hear the voice
Of thy gentle Judge, and for thy toil rejoicing:
'Come, my most faithful servant, enter in
The kingdom of the Father everlasting.'
That day, remember me, and say:
'O Christ most gentle,
Have mercy on a poor man, Alcuin.'
And now,
Beside the shore of the sail-winged sea
I wait the coming of God's silent dawn.
Do thou help this my journey with thy prayer.
I ask this, with a devoted heart.

More Latin Lyrics

There was something of the Blessed Alcuin about Stephen Gwynn, who died in peace on 11 June, as did Lord Abbot Alcuin on 19 May more than 1,100 years ago. There was the same humility, the same high pride, the indulgence towards all young creatures, the humanity in scholarship, the exquisite gift for verse, the fisherman's love of trout streams, the life-long devotion to France and her wines, the ancient courtesy, the faith kept with their friends. Gwynn, like Alcuin, had the European mind, but they knew their own as well: at bed-rock level Alcuin was a man of York, sprung from the field and rock above Spurn Head; and Gwynn a son of the O'Briens and of a rectory in Donegal. It was Charlemagne who called Alcuin 'Horace', and it might well have been Stephen's middle name; but the iron that was in Horace as well as the amenity was in these two also. Alcuin could withstand Charlemagne to his face; and Stephen Gwynn, classical scholar and M.P. for Galway, enlisted as a private in 1915 and was in the trenches in Flanders at the age of 51. To Alcuin in his old age among the vineyards of Touraine came the vision of the white-winged sea; for Stephen Gwynn, dying in Dublin,

> Few roads and far to grey Glencar,
> Where Curragh ripples past.

The Times, 19 June 1950

117 THOU REMAINEST
(*Heb. 1.11*)

BOETHIUS

O Thou whose reason guides the universe,
Maker of earth and heaven,
Who from eternity dost send forth Time
And thyself motionless
Givst all things power to move.
No cause outside thyself prevailed on Thee
To fashion floating matter to a world,
But an instinctive pattern in thy mind.
Utterly good, and with no taint of malice
Thou didst fashion all things in that heavenly mould.
Thou the supreme in beauty, carrying
A world of beauty in thy mind, didst shape
A perfect whole and bade it then release
Its perfect parts: numbered the elements,

184

That cold might contain fire, and dryness water:
Lest fire too pure might vanish into air,
Or weight of water drag down flooded earth.
O Father, give the spirit power to climb
To the fountain of all light, and be purified.
Break through the mists of earth, the weight of the clod,
Shine forth in splendour, Thou that art calm weather,
And quiet resting place for faithful souls.
To see Thee is the end and the beginning,
Thou carriest us, and Thou dost go before,
Thou art the journey, and the journey's end.

More Latin Lyrics

118 THOU HAST LOOSED MY BONDS
(*Ps. 116.16*)

GEORGE RUSSELL (Æ)

Long ago a *Times* reviewer described Æ among the other writing men and politicians as a 'gentle giant among pygmies', and again of a book of his that came out in the Troubles of 1917, that it was the far off piping of a flute on a mountainside. He is perhaps the only figure of our time who makes credible the legends of the saints: St Kevin who used to pray with his hands held out through the window of his hut, and a bird nested in his hand, and the kind saint would not disturb her till the young ones were hatched: and the other saint reading a heavy book, and a stag came by and knelt and offered its antlers as a reading-desk. For though he rebelled against many things in his youth and wrote what he now calls 'flaming rhetoric' on the right of the soul 'still to persist, still to defy, still to obey the orders of another captain, that unknown deity within, whose trumpet call sounds louder than all the cries of men'. 'I wrote so fiercely,' he says, 'because the idea of revolt had incinerated in the hot body of youth, ... and I did not then know that wisdom lies in the *transmutation* or reconcilement of opposites, and *were we gentle enough*, then God would give us a star to lead.'

He has been likened to the Indian mystics because of his strange powers of withdrawal, his moments of vision and his trances of

185

meditation: but there is *one* difference that sets a gulf between them. He has *never* so lost himself in the contemplation of beauty or of God that he has forgotten men: and the only man of our time who has the apocalyptic vision and prophetic fire of Blake, has not contented himself with writing magical verse or putting on canvas the strange presences that lighten the dark for him: he has pedalled up and down Ireland on his old bicycle, persuading the farmers to new ways; and spent his days in an office over statistics of creameries and the milk yield of cows. One furious and romantic young man even wrote of him that he had 'taken the stones of the altar of Irish liberty and built them into cowbyres.' Æ would probably admit it, for to him 'the day cometh, and now is, when neither on this mountain nor at Jerusalem shall men worship the Father', and as in one of his most characteristic pictures, above a man in a wet field planting cabbages there stands the figure of a prince archangel.

For the two divine visitations of his boyhood have been the openings from which his whole life drew. One, when he lay 'on the hill of Kilmasheogue and Earth revealed itself to me as a living thing, and rock and clay were made transparent, so that I saw lordlier and lovelier beings than I had known before, and was made partner in memory of mighty things happening in ages long sunken behind time.' The other, again in boyhood 'when I was living in the country and was told of a woman who was dying, how a quarter of an hour or so before she went, she wept that she was unable to rise and nurse a sick neighbour: and there came on me a transfiguring anguish because of this self-forgetfulness of hers, and though the mood was too high for me to sustain, and I passed from it to many egoisms, yet this was the starting-point of whatever selflessness was in my life.'

It was in the early days of the Irish Agricultural Organization Society that Yeats suggested to Plunkett and Anderson that the man they wanted was Æ. Yeats spoke of him as a poet and a saint yet with extraordinary practical gifts, a saint who would not preach, but some unconscious virtue went out of him. So Æ came to them, 'and they saw a man in no way corresponding to Yeats' description of him.'

They saw a tall thin man, overflowing with wild humour: the ends of his eyes went up and he seemed to them like a kindly satyr, something that had not yet experienced civilization, for the first stipulation was that he should not receive more than £3 a week. No man's work, according to him, was worth more.

'They gave him a bicycle,' George Moore goes on,

186

and he rode through Ireland, preaching the doctrine of co-operation and dairy-farming from village to village. As soon as he arrived in the village, everybody's heart became a little warmer, and a little friendlier: the sensation of isolation and loneliness which all human beings feel thawed a little: everybody must have felt happier the night that that kindly man mounted the platform, threw back his hair and began to talk to them, giving them shrewd advice and making them feel that he loved them, and that they were not unworthy of his love. The only house in the poor village in which he could lodge would be the priest's house, and the lonely village priest who does not meet a friend with whom he can exchange an idea once in three months, would spend a memorable evening with Æ. The priests in those villages have little bookshelves along their room, and Æ would go to these shelves and find a book that had not interested the priest since the enthusiasm of his youth had died down: he would open this book and read passages and awaken the heart of the priest. In the morning the old bicycle would be brought out, and away Æ would go, and the priest I am sure looked after him, sorry that he was going. Protestant, Catholic, Presbyterian, Methodist, all united in loving Æ. It is the mission of some men to enable their fellows to live beyond themselves, and Æ possesses the power to an extraordinary degree.

I suppose that George Moore is the subtlest, most delicately malicious writer of our time: and it is the measure of Æ's greatness that it has compelled even Moore to write like an evangelical. Æ himself protested that Moore had made him the hero of a school-girl novel, had let him have no single human failing: and Moore replied that he could find none, none at any rate that mattered. St Francis of Assisi was ugly, but no man thought so when he had seen his eyes.

Unpublished notebook, August 1935

119 **NEW AND OLD**
(*Matt. 13.52*)

TRIBUTE TO BASIL BLACKETT

PRUDENTIUS

Black clouds and mists and sullen night –
This world's confused and murky gloom –
Disperse – begone – the Dawn is come:
Christ enters: in the East is light.

More blest is he, who maimed from strife,
Each limb unruly cut away,
Wasted and lamed, when comes the day,
Is called to enter into life . . .

Of the four poets represented in his translations, St Gregory Nazianzen had long been Basil Blackett's familiar. His absorption in Byzantine Greek was hereditary; himself the eldest son, he had been called after Basil of Caesarea – St Gregory's arbitrary friend; a younger brother, Clement, narrowly escaped Eusebius. His signature follows his father's in a squat edition of the Septuagint, written and dated in an immature hand. It was the day of his father's funeral; he was eleven years of age. The book went back with him to school, a kind of reliquary: from that day, too, the future Controller of Finance at the Treasury and Finance Member for India took the auditing of the family budget on his small but stocky shoulders.

It was in 1920, while he was still at the Treasury, that the Nazianzen translations were written; those from medieval Latin belong to the months before his death. Of the Latin poets, Prudentius, born of Pyrenean, as Basil of Northumbrian, border stock, was like him a public servant, though of the older Rome: at fifty-seven he renounced the world. Hildebert, the scholar bishop of Le Mans, was forced by William Rufus into the undying quarrel between Church and State, and half a century before Becket, found in it prison and exile. Saint Peter Damian, a passionate lover of the pagan learning, renounced it for a hermit's cell, and must in turn renounce his cell for the Cardinal-Bishopric of Ostia and the searing work of Hildebrand's reforms. Gregory Nazianzen, scholar and contemplative, was harried his life

188

long by administration and public clamour, culminating in his brief
patriarchate of Byzantium. Not one of them but wrote out of some
tension of the spirit.

PETER DAMIAN

For the springs of living waters pants my parched soul athirst:
Still my spirit, prison'd, exiled, longs its bars of flesh to burst,
Straining, yearning, pining, burning for the home it knew at first.

Here it moaneth and it groaneth, faint with sin, by care fordone;
In surrender sees the splendour of the glory that is gone:
Sting of present sorrow sharpens memory of bliss foreknown.

To these four came a man of a thousand contradictions — a thousand
warring impulses, of towering ambition and complete self-abnegation, a
humanist tempted by asceticism, a conservative rooted in the past,
driven by an *arduus furor* to amend the bitter present, a statesman
without office, a heretic in finance whose heresy is now orthodoxy, a
ruthless logical scientific brain overshadowed by the cloud of
unknowing, a sceptic apprehended by God .... These fragments of
translation are in a sense his autobiography: the struggle of his maturity
with the Angel, in which a man must lose 'the rebel strength by which he
fought' ('yet not without the anguish of the struggle', wrote John of
Salisbury, 'shall the face of truth be seen ... nor shall the day break
without a benediction'): his passion for the absolute in Peter Damian's
vision of the utter fulfilment of man's desire: the preoccupation of his
later years with the philosophy behind the idea of the Incarnation in
Hildebert's meditation on the taking of the manhood into God: Gregory
Nazianzen's final vision of Godhead that burns out all knowledge of a
man's self, *when all love, all longing, all desire, all seeking, all thoughts of
ours, all that we hope, shall be God.*

Read beside these, the articles of his political faith become themselves
a religion. His conviction of England's destiny—

Rome the flail becomes physician
Of a warring world's unease,

of a *Pax Britannica* deeper and more lasting than the Roman Peace,
because no longer cramped within a single citizenship: currency the
channel instead of the wall of partition: the freedom of the individual in
the planned State: these, his continual preoccupations, were his version

of Augustine's *Civitas Dei*. His faith was summed up in the last sentences he ever wrote, the concluding paragraph of a lecture to be delivered at Heidelberg, on the road which he died. 'Planning is "out of Marxianism, by the theory of evolution". Those two currents of thought interrupted the flow of the stream which had its source in the Christian and Platonic doctrine of the unique value of the individual soul. Planning must go back to that source before it can do its full service to the twentieth century world. The goal in view must be ... more freedom for the spiritual and intellectual individuality of all. Planning is valid only if it brings freedom for that part of man which lives in the realm of mind and spirit.' That freedom he sought and still seeks.

PETER DAMIAN

Christ who art the soldier's palm-wreath, bring me to Thy city blest:
Let me enter there, Thy veteran, and unarm at Thy behest,
To receive my portion there, and dwell with Thine elect at rest.
Grant me strength to battle on undaunted in this ceaseless war:
Grant me peace when I have fought my fight and earthly life is o'er:
Be my guerdon to possess Thee utterly for evermore.

Surely, whereso'er the body, must the eagles gather there:
One the Bread and One the Body which the Saints and Angels share:
Citizens of Earth and Heaven thus their unity declare.

No man, he once said, could ask a better dismission than the ancient epitaph: 'After he had served his own generation by the will of God, he fell on sleep, and was gathered to his fathers'. He had thirty years of that service behind him when he died unconscious at Marburg on 15 August 1935: but to those, and they were in many countries, who had looked to see

the harvest home
At the threshing on the floor of Rome,

it seemed that his sun had indeed set at right declensions and made but winter arches, so vast was the energy of knowledge and vision that had suddenly flared into darkness.

> ... *caduca patent nostris, aeterna negantur*
> *visibus.*

190

'Earth to earth, but be thou heaven's familiar, and let thine eyes depart not from those high places. For when this house of thine falls in ruins about thee, they shall abide thy coming, familiar roofs of home. No unknown stranger shalt thou climb there, where waits thee the place and the banner of thy star.'

Privately printed, 1937

120 THE REST OF THE HOLY SABBATH
(*Exod. 16.23*)

PETER ABELARD

How mighty are the Sabbaths,
How mighty and how deep,
That the high courts of heaven
To everlasting keep.
What peace unto the weary,
What pride unto the strong,
When God in whom are all things
Shall be all things to men.

Jerusalem is the city
Of everlasting peace,
A peace that is surpassing
And utter blessedness;
Where finds the dreamer waking
Truth beyond dreaming far,
Nor is the heart's possessing
Less than the heart's desire.

But ours, with minds uplifted
Unto the heights of God,
With our whole heart's desiring,
To take the homeward road,
And the long exile over,
Captive in Babylon,
Again unto Jerusalem,
To win at last return.

There Sabbath unto Sabbath
Succeeds eternally,
The joy that has no ending
Of souls in holiday.
And never shall the rapture
Beyond all mortal ken
Cease from the eternal chorus
That angels sing with men.

Now to the King Eternal
Be praise eternally,
From whom are all things, by whom
And in whom all things be.
From Whom, as from the Father,
By Whom, as by the Son,
In Whom, as in the Spirit,
God the Lord, Three in One.

Mediaeval Latin Lyrics

Biographical Notes

ABELARD, PETER (1079–1142) dominates the opening decades of the twelfth century as Master in the Schools of Paris (where John of Salisbury sat at his feet) until 1118, when his passion for the young and brilliant Heloise led to his undoing. When the discord finally resolved itself into harmony, the monk Peter Abelard wrote for Heloise, ábbess of the Paraclete, the *Liber Hymnorum*, a sequence of ninety-three liturgical hymns, thus inaugurating a new period of great Christian hymnody.

ALCUIN (c.735–804). It is difficult to overestimate Alcuin, who has never received from his own nation the fame he deserves. Much against his will, he gave up the headmastership of the School of York at fifty years of age at the request of the Emperor Charlemagne, in order to carry the learning that stemmed from Jarrow, Lindisfarne and the early Irish monks, to Aachen and thence to the whole of Europe. He reformed the liturgical calendar, secured a lasting pattern of worship, collated the Vulgate Bible, compiled text and music for eighteen masses, wrote military marches for the imperial troops, and as ábbot of Tours for the last eight years of his life, perfected the Caroline minuscule, pattern of modern Roman typefaces.

AUSONIUS (c.310–395) occupied a chair of rhetoric at twenty-five, at fifty was imperial tutor, at sixty-nine held the consulship, and seemed to lead a charmed life but for two sharp and abiding sorrows: the death of his wife when she was still 'the little lass'; and the emptiness and silence that descended on the close friendship between himself and his favourite pupil Paulinus of Nola, when the latter became a Christian and exchanged the leisure and luxury of life in Bordeaux for the stern asceticism of a life devoted to the homeless and underprivileged of Southern Italy.

BEDE, ST (c.673–735) is a Doctor of the Church, historian and chronologist, to whom we owe our custom of dating events from the birth of Christ, namely Anno Domini. He was the moving spirit behind the foundation of the famous School of York established by Egbert, his most eminent disciple. Alcuin became headmaster until, at Charlemagne's request, he took over the Palace school at Aachen where he trained Hrabanus Maurus. Hrabanus carried the York tradition to Fulda, the monastery founded by Bede's Devonshire contemporary Boniface, apostle of Germany, and from Fulda, Walafrid Strabo bore it to Reichenau.

BERNARD SYLVESTRIS (12c.) has never been completely identified, but modern research has pretty well established that he was a master of Tours, not of Chartres. He was certainly the author of *De mundi universitate*, a mixture of Platonist philosophy and natural history which, to judge from over twenty-five extant copies, was a mediaeval best-seller. Helen Waddell quotes him extensively as one of her favourite writers.

BLACKETT, BASIL PHILLOTT (1882–1935) a close friend whom Helen Waddell addressed as 'Abelard' was educated at Marlborough and University College, Oxford, before entering the Treasury in 1904. For six years, 1922–8, he was Finance Minister under two Governor-Generals of India. Many of the outstanding politicians of the day met at his house in London: it was he who introduced Stanley Baldwin to Helen. Basil Blackett was accidentally killed at a level crossing when driving to deliver a lecture at Heidelberg. Helen selected some of his translations from Greek and Latin poetry, and added the appreciation accompanying them, for circulation among his family and intimate friends.

BOETHIUS, ST SEVERINUS (480–c.524) has influenced the thought of Western Europe as few others have done. His famous Latin work, *De consolatione philosophiae*, embodying the subtle and precise Greek terminology of Plato and Aristotle, was the most widely-read book of the Middle Ages after the Bible. To him, human friendship was 'the most precious treasure in the world', a view taken up and shared by Christian humanists such as Alcuin in the 8th century, John of Salisbury in the 12th, Thomas More in the 16th. When Boethius incurred the displeasure of the Emperor Theodoric, he was consigned to a dungeon, tortured, and finally put to death. Throughout it all, he steadied his mind and soul on the thought of eternity, and remained unafraid.

COLUMBA, ST (524–597). Born in Donegal of a noble family, he was trained in the monastic life by St Finnian and left his native land about 563 with twelve companions to settle on the island of Iona. From there they evangelized the surrounding peoples, built churches and monasteries, and made the island a centre of Celtic Christianity, famous for its learning. His poem *Dies irae* derives from St Jerome's Vulgate translation of the prophet Zephaniah, and was to influence each generation until, in Helen Waddell's phrase, in the *Dies irae* of the Franciscan Thomas of Celano (1190–1260) 'it burns through the inmost veil of heaven.'

COLUMBANUS, ST (543–615), Abbot, educated at Bangor, Co. Down, was a monk of great holiness and learning. Like so many wandering Irish scholars, he felt the apostolic urge to evangelize. With the help of twelve fellow monks, he founded over one hundred monasteries throughout Europe, some of them becoming the most famous strongholds of Christian culture on the Continent.

EPHRAEM, ST (c.306–373). Doctor of the Church, biblical exegete, theologian and hymnographer, his writings have become very influential in the years following upon the Second Vatican Council when the importance of the early Syriac church is increasingly evident.

FULBERT OF CHARTRES, ST (c.960–1028), 'the very little bishop of a very great church' was regarded, contrary to his own self-evaluation, as a very embodiment of Socrates and Plato. A student at Reims under the famous Gerbert, he was appointed first as chancellor of the cathedral school at Chartres, and later became bishop. He made the school of Chartres the most distinctive in Europe: he had a talent for attracting genius, so that the tradition he established persisted long after his own death. Of his many accomplishments none is more delightful than his musicianship: he not only wrote songs but set them to accompaniments on the lyre, the monochord and the organ – how his students must have loved him! He was also not above composing adroitly-rhymed teasing skits on his companions' foibles.

HILDEBERT OF LAVARDIN (1056–1133), an outstanding classical scholar and one of the finest hymnologists of his age was, above all, a noble and saintly Christian bishop, first of Le Mans in 1096 until 1125 when he was appointed Archbishop of Tours. Under William Rufus, a powerful opponent, Hildebert suffered exile, imprisonment and disgrace. An ardent defender of the Church's freedom, St Bernard saluted him as a pillar of the Church, and John of Salisbury ranked him with the classical writers of antiquity for his purity of style.

HRABANUS MAURUS (776–856) moved from the abbey of Fulda to Tours, to profit from the tuition of Alcuin, who loved him and called him Maurus after St Benedict's favourite disciple. In 822 he was elected abbot of Fulda, an office he found distasteful – 'seeing that these young ones have enough to eat is a great hindrance to one's reading.' Retiring, to his relief, from the abbatial office, he spent seven halcyon years in bible study, theology and poetry until his appointment in 847 to the Archiepiscopal See of Mainz, his birthplace. Such was his spiritual stature that the Emperor Lothair said of him, 'If God gave my predecessors Jerome and Augustine and Ambrose, He gave me Hrabanus.'

JOHN OF SALISBURY (c.1115–1180), the outstanding humanist of the 12th century, went to Paris as an indigent young student where he sat at Abelard's feet. He then entered the service of the Papal Curia, was attached to the household of Archbishop Theobald of Canterbury, and on the latter's death served his successor, Thomas Becket, whom he strongly supported against King Henry II. In 1176 John became Bishop of Chartres. Four years later, he died as poor as he had lived, bequeathing to his cathedral his dearest possessions: all his books and a phial of the blood of the blessed martyr St Thomas Becket, shed on that fatal 29 December 1170, when John, his secretary, stood in Canterbury Cathedral, powerless to prevent the crime.

LANGTON, STEPHEN (1151–1228), Cardinal and Archbishop of Canterbury, theologian, historian, poet and statesman, ranks as one of the most illustrious of mediaeval churchmen. To him we owe the division of the Bible into chapters, the Magna Carta, and the Code of Canon Law. His sequence, *Veni, Sancte Spiritus,* sung to this day in the mass of Whit Sunday, was praised by a contemporary Cistercian monk as being the work of 'Master Stephen de Langton, a man worthy of respect for his life and learning.'

MARBOD OF RENNES (c.1035–1123), one of the most eminent classical scholars of the eleventh century, was also a true poet. After a distinguished career in the Church, he died aged eighty-eight as a simple monk in the monastery of St Aubin in Angers, the city of his birth.

MILTON, JOHN (1608–1674) needs no introduction. In August 1638, Charles Diodati, a young doctor of medicine and Milton's closest friend from their schooldays together at St Paul's, died in London, probably of the plague. Milton, in Italy at the time, knew nothing of his friend's untimely end until his return home, when Diodati was already a year in his grave. The poet chose to hide his intense personal grief behind a mask of the Latin pastoral of lament, his *Epitaphium Damonis*. Three centuries later, in 1942, Helen Waddell translated Milton's elegy as an expression of her own deep suffering at the loss, during the Second World War, of Jack and George Martin, the dearly-loved nephews for whose instruction and delight she had told the bible stories which were later to be published as *Stories from Holy Writ*.

PAULINUS OF NOLA, ST (c.355–431), son of the Prefect of Gaul and overlord of vast estates in Italy, caused heartbreak to Ausonius, his old tutor, when after a short brilliant career he received Christian baptism in 390 and interpreted his faith in terms of radical renunciation. About 395, with his Spanish wife Theresia, he retired to Nola, a little town near Naples. Here they built a church, an aqueduct for fresh water, and housed and fed outcasts and beggars. Elected Bishop of Nola in 409, Paulinus spent the remainder of his life in poverty, prayer and pastoral work. Of his numerous poems, only thirty-two survive.

PETER DAMIAN, ST (1007–1072), monk, bishop, cardinal, and stern ascetic, he was Pope Gregory VII's right-hand man, his 'holy Satan' as the Pope teasingly called him, in the reform of the many abuses within the Church. His prolific doctrinal writings and eloquent preaching, his integrity and obvious sanctity, established him as a spiritual force in his own lifetime. Never formally canonized, he was declared a Doctor of the Church in 1828.

PETRONIUS ARBITER (20–66) was possibly a native of Marseilles and author of the *Satyricon*, the first European novel, and was surprisingly, perhaps, John of Salisbury's favourite author. At first a member of the Emperor Nero's intimate circle, he incurred his displeasure, and was condemned to death on a false charge. However, he outwitted his accusers by slitting his own veins and appearing to fall asleep during a banquet, to the strains of a first-century programme of light music and verse.

PRUDENTIUS (348–c.410): saluted as the Virgil and Horace of the Christians, he was probably a native of Saragossa, and a contemporary of Jerome, Ambrose and Augustine. He rose to high judicial office under Emperor Theodosius, but at fifty-seven withdrew from civil administration to follow in obscurity his Christian calling. His long and simple yet profound poems exerted a powerful influence over the Middle Ages; his liturgical cycle of hymns is the glory of the Roman breviary.

RADBOD (d.917), the son of a Frankish noble, chose to link his studies with the tradition of the school of York and Alcuin by going to Tours to prepare for his future under the direction of Abbot Hugh of St Martin's. In 899 he was elected Bishop of Utrecht but, after a stormy episcopate, died in exile. (Helen Waddell points out that the Zwendebold of his epitaph was King of Lorraine, and illegitimate son of Arnulf, one of the last of Charlemagne's house.)

SEDULIUS SCOTTUS, an unknown Irish scholar – one of many – who ended up at Liège, tempest-tossed and sodden in a scurry of sleet some time after the year 840, and was given warm hospitality, food, a bed and safe lodging as the bishop's *scholasticus*, for Hartgar recognized a fine Greek scholar when he met one. Helen Waddell came across his name in 1924 when working at the British Museum, and wrote in some excitement to her sister Meg: 'Scot means Irish in the Middle Ages, and Sedulius is Latin for Sheil. He came to be schoolmaster at Liège . . . Do you wonder it took me in the legs?'

THEODULF OF ORLEANS (c.750–821). A native of Saragossa who attracted Charlemagne's attention; he was made Abbot of Fleury and Bishop of Orleans. He is best known as the author of the hymn for Palm Sunday, *Gloria laus et honor*, which has passed into liturgical use. He was the leading theologian and poet of the Frankish empire. Helen Waddell considered that there was nothing in the whole of Carolingian verse worthy to stand by his poem in this anthology.

THOMAS AQUINAS, ST (c.1225–1274), the greatest of the Schoolmen, was placed by Dante with Boethius and Bede in the circle of twelve lights revolving with dance and song in the heaven of the sun. But whether St Thomas was author of the *Adoro te* is a disputed question: Helen thought he was, and for present purposes that must suffice.

WALAFRID STRABO, 'the squinter' (809–849), was a monk of Reichenau, a house founded by Irish monks in 724. He was sent to study under Hrabanus Maurus at Fulda where he imbibed the English monastic tradition that stemmed from York. In 838 he was elected abbot of his own monastery, for by then his obvious genius was acknowledged. At barely eighteen his long poem *Visio Wettinis* forestalled Dante in a curious fashion: Walafrid had taken down the story himself from the lips of a dying monk at Reichenau. It was there, as abbot, that he created his garden and sent his book on gardening to Grimold, abbot of St Gall. Although during his short life he wrote a great number of works, scriptural, theological and poetical, it is his work *Of Gardening*, printed in this anthology, that is still green while the tomes of theology gather dust. Death claimed him at the age of forty, when he was drowned, says his epitaph, 'crossing the thirsty sands of the Loire' – a fitting though untimely end for a poet.

Acknowledgements and Sources

The editor and publishers are grateful to Constable Publishers and Mary M. Martin for permission to reproduce copyright material and to Mrs Honor Sharman for her gracious loan of Helen Waddell's tribute to Sir Basil Blackett, her mother's brother.

Quotations from Helen Waddell's printed works, published by Constable:
Lyrics from the Chinese (ed., 1913)
The Wandering Scholars (1927)
Mediaeval Latin Lyrics (1929)
Peter Abelard: A Novel (1933)
Beasts and Saints (1934)
The Desert Fathers (1936)
Stories from Holy Writ (1949)

More Latin Lyrics: From Virgil to Milton ed. Felicitas Corrigan. Victor Gollancz, 1976.

'John of Salisbury' from *Essays and Studies*, vol. xiii, ed. Caroline Spurgeon. Oxford, Clarendon Press, 1928.

'Scholares Vagantes' from *The Heritage*. Published on behalf of the Four Women's Colleges in Oxford, January 1925